The Roa
Gui

England and Wales

Dick Henneman

Panther Publishing

First published by Panther Publishing Ltd in 2004
Panther Publishing Ltd, 10 Lime Avenue, High Wycombe, Bucks. HP11 1DP, UK

Acknowledgements

I'd like to thank all those who knowingly or unknowingly have helped me in the preparation of this guide. In particular to my wife Shirley and our daughter Jo who have accompanied me on many of the routes, and to Roger, Mark, Shaz, Simon and Rob who have all put up with my disappearing down unmarked roads just to find out 'what it's like down there'. They've all suffered many a U-turn as a consequence. And thanks too to Ron Brett and Brettours who kindled my enthusiasm for long distance touring and exploring all those hard to find roads and places.

Dick Henneman

ISBN 0 9535098 6 9

Contents

About This Guide iv
Introduction to England and Wales 1
A Potted History 1
Geography & Geology 3
Climate 4
Communications 5
  Postal Services 5
  Telephones 5
Documentation 6
Insurance 6
  Personal and Medical Cover 6
  Vehicle Recovery 7
Riding and the Law 7
Maps and Information 8
Fuel 8
Going Touring 9
The Right Bike 9
Planning the Trip 9
Clothing 10
Other Essentials 11
Luggage 12
  Hard Luggage 12
  Soft Luggage 13
Bike Preparation 15
England On Two Wheels 17
Geography 17
Getting There 18
What to See 19
Accommodation and Information 20
Roads and Routes 23
Map of England Showing Routes 25
Wales On Two Wheels 76
Geography 76
Getting There 77
What to See 77
Accommodation and Information 77
Map of Wales Showing Routes 79
Index 114

Roads and Routes - England
Southwest
  1 Launceston to Okehampton 26
  2 Taunton to South Molton 28
  3 Taunton to Lynmouth 30
  4 Lynmouth to Bridgewater 32
  5 Nunney to Taunton 34
South and South East
  6 Hungerford to Westbury 36
  7 Reading to Andover 38
  8 Newbury to Calne 40
Midlands
  9 Streatley to Lechlade 42
  10 Postcombe to Bicester 44
  11 Lechlade to Daventry 46
  12 Kidlington to Ryton 48
  13 Bedford to Catworth 50
  14 Islip to Corby 52
East Anglia
  15 Mildenhall to Outwell 54
  16 Thetford to King's Lynn 56
North
  17 Ashbourne to Ladybower Resv'r. 58
  18 Sheffield to Glossop 60
  19 Barnard Castle to Alston 62
  20 Alston to Penrith 64
  21 Carlisle to Kendal 66
  22 Kendal to Leyburn 68
  23 Leyburn to Ripon 70
  24 Carterway Heads to Middleton 72
  25 Bishop Auckland to Jedburgh 74

Roads and Routes - Wales
  26 Chepstow to Usk 80
  27 Usk to Raglan 84
  28 Talgarth to Beaufort 84
  29 Brecon to Beulah 86
  30 Brecon to Builth Wells 88
  31 Llanwrtyd Wells to Tregaron 90
  32 Rhayader to Devil's Bridge 92
  33 Rhayader to Devil's Bridge (Elan) 94
  34 Machynlleth to Llanidloes 96
  35 Tywyn to Minffordd 98
  36 Machynlleth to Dolgellau (A470) 100
  37 Machynlleth to Dolgellau (A487) 102
  38 Dolgellau to Barmouth 104
  39 Dinas Mawddwy to Bala 106
  40 Trawsfynydd to Bala 108
  41 Porthmadog to Llanberis 110
  42 Betws-Y-Coed to Menai Bridge 112

About This Guide

This is a touring guide book for motorcyclists. If you enjoy getting about on two-wheels, whether it's on a tourer, a traillie, a sportsbike, a cruiser or a classic, then you can go touring. And in spite of all the speed restrictions, Gatso cameras and general traffic mayhem, England and Wales still have some great roads for the motorcyclist to ride.

If your idea of travelling is finding the most interesting way from A to B, with good demanding riding, places to take a break along the way, and excellent scenery, then this is a book for you. But if you're more interested in how quickly you can get to B and what you'll find when you get there, then you'd be better off reading one of the more 'conventional' guide books.

This book is intended to persuade you to go touring, and once you've tried it I've no doubt that you'll want to go back for more. So as well as information on the variety of features in the country itself, I've included sections on preparation for both yourself and the bike, how to get there (and back) on two wheels, and the types of accommodation that are available and how to book. But most important of all, there are details and routes for some of the best and most interesting roads and routes for you to ride.

This is the first edition of the guide, and everything in it is based upon my own experiences. However, in an area the size of England and Wales things are constantly changing and nothing in the guide should be taken as a guarantee that what you'll find is exactly as described. In particular, road works and improvements are common and may make some of the routes out-of-date before they can be put in print. You can help me here, by letting me know what you find 'on the ground' and I'll then incorporate this in the next edition. In addition, if you find some great routes or services and facilities that would help other motorcyclists then I'd like to hear about these as well.

Enjoy!

Dick Henneman

October 2003

Your Introduction to England and Wales

England and Wales are two of the countries that make up the United Kingdom, a collection of islands and countries, perched above France and surrounded by the North Sea, the English Channel and the North Atlantic. The UK covers an area of some 121,000 sq. miles (312,000 sq. km.), and England and Wales occupy some 48% of this landmass, but are home to around 82% of the total population. This means that things can get a little busy at times on the roads, especially in England, which has over 20 million registered vehicles on its books and some serious traffic congestion in places. This is especially the case in the south and southeast of England, and in and around the major cities, towns and industrial areas. And if that's not enough, there's been a recent proliferation of Gatso speed cameras and 50 mph speed restrictions that seem to be spreading like a rash across the countryside.

Now you're probably thinking that for a book that's all about the enjoyment of riding motorbikes on the open road, this isn't a great introduction. But you'd be wrong.

There's a tremendous amount of England and Wales that's still a pleasure to ride and explore from the seat of a motorbike. All you need is a little bit of local knowledge and some forward planning, and that's where this guide can help. In it I've collected some of the roads that I've enjoyed riding, either for the scenery that they pass through, or the dynamics of the riding itself, or sometimes both. But this is not a definitive list. There are some great roads that I've ridden that I'm not going to tell you about – well, not just yet anyway – and there are a lot more out there just waiting for you to discover. So get out there.

A Potted History

So how did England and Wales get to be the way they are now?

As the glaciers retreated from the landscape for the last time some 10,000 years ago, Stone Age men pushed trails though the virgin forests that advanced in the wake of the ice. These early Britons came across the land bridge that joined the country to the rest of continental Europe, until the North Sea broke through some 3,000 years later. Neolithic invaders from the Mediterranean lands replaced Stone Age man, and brought with them farming techniques, the art of pottery and the use of stone. They worked flints and were buried in long barrows which are scattered on the Downs across the south of England and in other parts of the country. Later invaders bought skills in the working of bronze, and were responsible for the erection of enormous stones circles from Salisbury Plain to the Orkney Islands.

At this time, Britain was known only as a faraway land at the uncertain frontier of the world, wrapped in mists and mystery. But this wasn't to remain the case for much longer. Around 500 BC. came the first of many great migratory movements from the people of the continental land mass, fuelled by increasing population pressures around the Rhine. These were the Celts, who bought with them a new technology based on the working of iron. Later Celts were miners and traders, farmers, horse-breeders and cattle farmers, and the Celtic language they used still lives on in the Welsh tongue.

The Roman invasion that began in AD. 43 was not a mass migration, but an occupation by a small group of highly organised conquerors. The Romans subjugated the natives, used their resources, and dominated them with superior force and administration. The native Celtic groups, in alliance with Germanic raiders from across the North Sea finally broke the Roman hold after some 400 years and set up Anglo-Saxon settlements all across the English plain. They in turn then faced the onslaught of the Norse and Danish invaders, who established bases in the Shetlands and Orkneys and then spread down the west coast. Another group of Norsemen who had established themselves in France in an area that was to become Normandy, added French refinement to the hardiness of their Viking ancestors. The Saxons were no match for these Norman invaders, and after William's victory over Harold in 1066, the Normans overawed the population, by then some 2 million, by building a series of strongholds many of which still stand today. Close links with the continent led to the extension of monastic life, the building of new abbeys, the foundation of market towns and the emergence of great baronial estates.

With the Normans, the last successful military invaders of Britain, came the final major contribution to the evolution of a common language. The Latin and French elements combined with the Germanic and the Celtic to make the island tongue as complex in its origin as the physical characteristics of its people.

Throughout the Middle Ages there was a great deal of social change and upheaval as populations increased through gradual improvements in agriculture and animal husbandry, and the food surpluses over the immediate requirements of the producers allowed trade to develop and major population centres to be formed. Many of these were based upon settlements first established in Roman times, while others came about from feudal centres set up by Lords and Barons to manage their estates'. Some were created from markets held to sell and distribute the agriculture produce.

With subsistence-level farming left well behind there was time for some people to follow academic pursuits and for the development of trade and exploration. This led to the last major social upheaval of the Industrial Revolution that started slowly in the middle of 17th century, and reached its peak at the end of the 19th and the early part of the 20th centuries.

Geography & Geology

The variety of the British scenery is largely due to the influences of the underlying rocks. Some of these in the barren wilderness of West Sutherland in Scotland, date back around 3,400 million years and are the amongst the oldest rocks in the world; while others off the coast of Dungeness, are still in the process of being formed. But around 570 million years ago, most of what is now the UK was below a warm shallow sea and over a period of time a great thickness of mud and silt accumulated. This was compressed under later deposits, along with ash and lava from volcanoes, and then some 350 million years ago there was a major upwards earth movement which resulted in the formation of the Caledonian Mountains. The pressures that created these mountains also caused molten rock to flow into the mountain roots giving rise to granite and igneous intrusions, some of which are still visible in Snowdonia and the Lake District.

In the following Devonian period, many of these mountain uplifts were worn away by erosive forces and the area became a desert. Much red sandstone was formed about this time, before another sea incursion drowned everything out. While all this was going on, life had evolved in the seas, and the chalky remains of these tiny creatures formed thick layers of limestone. These in turn were covered by the deltas of great rivers, which then silted up, forming muddy swamps on which thick forests flourished, decayed, and were covered with mud, subsequently turning into coalfields.

The limestones that were laid down in the Jurassic period some 175 million years ago, form one long ridge that runs from the North Yorkshire Moors through the Cotswolds to the Isle of Purbeck, and are responsible for some of Britain's best building stone and most of its iron ore. From Salisbury Plain, chalk uplands radiate northeast along the Chilterns and on to Flamborough Head in Yorkshire. To the southeast the chalk forms the North and South Downs.

In west Scotland, the Tertiary Era which started around 65 million years ago, was marked by a new phase of volcanic activity which resulted in granites forming on the islands of Rhum, Eigg, Skye and Arran, and lava flows that formed the hexagonal columns of Fingal's Cave and the Giant's Causeway in Northern Ireland. In southern England, this period which resulted in the formation of the Alps on mainland Europe, folded up the land against more resistant blocks to the north and east. The crests of these upfolds were later worn away to leave the steep slopes of the North and South Downs.

The last great formative action that moulded the British landscape was the Ice Age that descended from the northeast around 1 million years ago. At its greatest extent some 200,000 years ago, a permanent ice sheet covered the land as far south as a line drawn from the Thames to the mouth of the Severn. Huge tongues of ice moved out from the highlands in the north on to the lowlands of the south and east Britain. The deep trough-like valleys of the Lake District and Snowdonia were all scoured out by these glaciers, and the vast amounts of material carried by the ice sheets were spread throughout the lowlands as hummocks of sand and gravel and great sheets of thick clay. The immense mass of water from the melting of the ice sheets resulted in a rise in sea levels that eventually separated Britain from the rest of Europe.

But the story hasn't quite finished yet. Hills and mountains are still being eroded and rivers continue to carry down material to the lowlands estuaries and the sea. The bed of the North Sea is slowly sinking under the weight of the new deposits, and the coast line of the southeast and the east coast is being continually attacked and eroded.

Climate

The British climate can never be accused of being dull. Awful on occasions, but dull - no. Lying between the land mass of Eurasia to the east and the watery expanse of the Atlantic Ocean to the west, the British weather depends very much on what is going on in these neighbouring areas. When westerly winds blow they bring the relative mildness of the ocean atmosphere at any time of the year. Easterlies however, bring different conditions according to the season.

Despite its reputation, Britain's climate and day-to-day weather conditions are relatively predictable. Over the Atlantic there is often a confrontation between cold airstreams moving south from the Arctic, and warm moisture-laden air moving north from the Tropics. This produces depressions - pockets of low air pressure - which move eastwards or north-eastwards across the ocean, often crossing Britain or brushing against its shores. Barometers fall, then rise again, as a mild windy and wet period is quickly followed by a warm dull spell or squally cold showers. At other times the zone of high pressure centred over the Azores expands northwards. Then, calmer air flows over the country, barometers rise and the weather is clear and sunny.

So now you're all meteorologists! But that's very much a simplification of the weather process and there's a lot of other factors that can cause considerable local variations.

Spring is normally the driest season even though April is traditionally showery. Halfway through the month the cold weather starts receding, and there are often some very warm days during the second half of the month. West-coast districts are popular for spring holidays as they are less vulnerable to rearguard actions from the winter. By late spring daytime, temperatures will have usually risen to around 21 - 24°C over a wide area. In May and June, maximum temperatures along the coasts usually exceed the sea-surface temperatures by around 5 - 9°C. This difference, at its greatest along the east coast, causes an alternation between on and offshore breezes.

June is the brightest month of the year in general, and the average daily sunshine ranges from eight hours in the extreme south, to about five hours in the north of Scotland. Rainfall tends to increase during July and August, partly because Atlantic depressions come nearer to the coasts during these months and partly because the air, as it becomes heated, is capable of holding more moisture.

Late summer is often noted for its very warm weather, and this may well continue into September with the eastern side of the country likely to be drier as the southwesterly winds will have lost a lot of their moisture as they travel across the country.

The autumn winds eventually move round to the west and northwest, and the weather becomes less settled. The air can be exceptionally clear during the sunnier spells. North and northwest winds often bring heavy falls of snow to the north of the country during late October or November, but these are usually short-lived, and when the winds subside and the sky clears the beauty of the countryside is unparalleled.

Communications

Throughout the whole of England and Wales communications are usually very good, although in the remoter areas there may be some delays. Most of us want to keep in touch when we're away, hopefully just so we can tell everyone at home what a wonderful time we're having. But it's also a good idea to leave some contact details with friends and family, just so they can get hold of you if necessary. Try to avoid leaving contact information with your employer, unless you're among the really dedicated. After all, you are supposed to be enjoying yourself!

Postal Services

Post Office® branches can be found in most small towns, a number of villages and in the cities, and are usually red in colour. The sign to look for is a red oval enclosing the words 'Post Office' in yellow. Opening hours vary with location, but generally are from 9.00am to 16.30pm with an hour for lunch taken sometime between 12.00pm and 14.00pm. Queues can be long, so if you only want the standard 1st and 2nd class stamps you can avoid the wait by purchasing them in books of six or twelve at most newsagents or stamp vending machines.

There are two standards of mail delivery, first and second class. First class mail is targeted for next day delivery on the mainland, with second class deliveries being made the day after. Look for large, red cylindrical post boxes on pavements and street corners, or smaller red boxes set into walls and brickwork. International mail is variable, and depends largely on the delivery at the destination. For anything urgent you should use first class mail, but if the package is important then you should always use registered post.

Telephones

Since the UK telephone service was opened to competition in the early 1980's, a number of service providers have appeared on the scene, and some have since vanished without trace. However the main operator in the public sector is still British Telecom and they run the majority of public call boxes. In Central London you will find other operators running call box telephone services, and there are cable network companies that also provide telephony services. Call boxes originally took coins, but more and more now take prepayment phone cards that can be purchased from newsagents and post offices. Some will take standard credit and debit cards, but you'll need to know your p.i.n. number in order to use them. However, away from the more populous areas coins are still mostly in use, with card/coin boxes beginning to appear in some places. To make an international call, dial 00 and when you get the tone, enter the country code followed by the area code and the number.

Useful country codes are:

34	Spain	32	Belgium
33	France	31	Netherlands
1	USA	49	Germany
353	Eire	41	Switzerland
39	Italy	351	Portugal

England and Wales have good coverage for mobile phone users. The four major network service providers are Vodafone, O_2 (formerly Cellnet), Orange, and T-Mobile (formerly One-2-One). All of them provide good reception in the cities and urban areas, but there are differences in the more rural areas. The current technology in use is GSM and most providers also offer a GPRS overlay service. If you're visiting from overseas, you should check with your service provider to see if they have a roaming agreement with a UK service provider, and make sure that you will be able to access the services you need along with any other arrangements that may be necessary. 3G mobile services are just starting to become available, but coverage at the moment is mostly restricted to the cities and major urban areas.

Documentation

In the UK there is no legal requirement to carry your vehicle and other personal documentation on you at all times. However, if you're stopped by a Police Officer or you're involved in an incident, you'll need to produce the appropriate documents at a Police Station within five days, so it's probably a good idea to have them with you, or at least back at where you're staying. And if you're visiting from abroad you should have your vehicle registration, insurance, and driver's licence documents with you as well as your passport.

Insurance

If you're travelling to England or Wales from Europe or even further afield, then you should check with your insurance company or broker to ensure that your insurance meets the minimum British requirements. For peace of mind you'd be well advised to have fully comprehensive cover especially if you're carrying a pillion. Again, your insurance company or broker will be able to advise and arrange any short term extensions to your policy.

Personal and Medical Cover

If you're a UK National and you're taken ill or suffer an injury while you're travelling around the country, then you can get medical attention under the National Health Service.

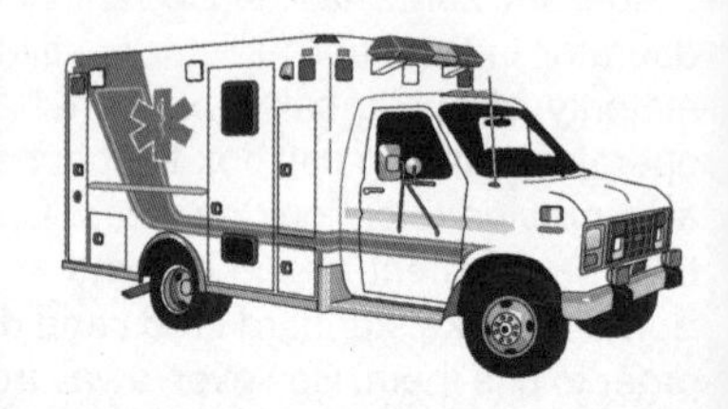

But if you're travelling from a country in the EC or from further afield, then you'd be recommended to take out an appropriate level of insurance cover that will pay for any treatment needed if you're taken ill, even to transport you home in an air-ambulance if the worst comes to the worst.

Vehicle Recovery

As well as taking out medical and accident insurance for yourself, you'd be well advised to take out cover for the bike as well. This will give you roadside assistance in case of a breakdown, get the parts to you that are needed for any repairs, and even get the bike back home when it's been damaged in an accident or if you're unable to ride it for whatever reason.

There are four major UK organisations offering both annual and short term cover and all these organisations also do travel insurance.:

RAC European Motoring Assistance	08705-722 722	www.rac.co.uk
AA Five Star	0800-085 2840	www.theaa.com
Green Flag	0800-3288 772	www.greenflag.com
Europ Assistance	01444-442038	

Overseas visitors should contact their local motoring organisations for UK breakdown cover arrangements before leaving home.

Riding and the Law

In the UK traffic travels on the left-hand side of the road, unlike the other countries in the European Community.

If you're visiting the country for the first time and have never driven on the left before, this may seem a little daunting but it soon becomes automatic. It's certainly a lot easier on two wheels than on four. The first few road junctions you come to will need to be thought about carefully, as will roundabouts, so be cautious – it's better than being dead or in hospital. You'll soon feel that riding on the left is the most natural thing to do, but be careful in the early days after you've been riding a good distance on a great piece of road with no junctions – and then you come to a crossroads only to find that your brain has slipped back into 'home-mode'.

Don't forget to switch back to the other side of the road when you get home. It sounds obvious, but . . . . .

As far as the British law on using motorcycles on the road is concerned, it shares many points with other countries. Here are some of the more interesting features.

- Safety helmets must be worn at all times by both the rider and the pillion.
- Black visors are currently illegal in the UK.
- Headlights do not need to be on when the bike is moving, but it's a good idea.
- The blood alcohol limit is 80mg. Make sure it's a lot, lot less.
- Speed limits in the UK are:

Motorways and Dual Carriageways	**112 kph**	**70 mph**
Other roads outside built-up areas	**96 kph**	**60 mph**
Towns and built-up areas	**48 kph**	**30 mph**

Unless speed limit signs are specifically marked otherwise.

Maps and Information

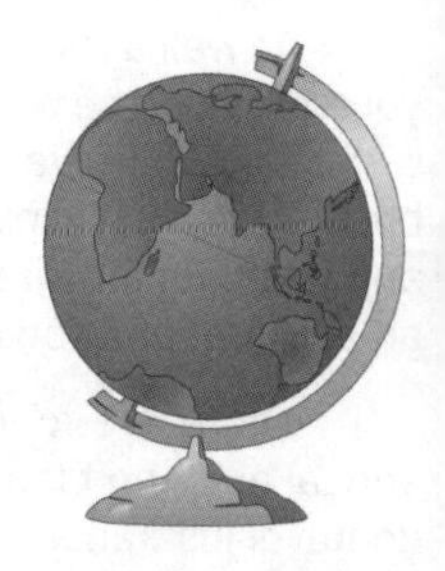

The UK is perhaps one of the most comprehensively mapped countries in the world, and the maps produced by the Ordnance Survey are some of the best around. The 1:50,000 series covers the whole of the country in superb detail, but the complete set is a little too bulky to carry around in most tank bags. Other large scale maps are available, and a useful version is the Geographer's A-to-Z Handy Road Atlas, as it's small enough to fit in most map pockets and the scale is just big enough to read while on the move. Also worth looking at is the Tuffmap road atlas of GB & Eire that's also in A5 format, but is printed on a tear-resistant and waterproof synthetic paper called Yupo.

Michelin produce a very useful series of 1:400,000 maps of theUK, and map sheets 502, 503 and 504 cover the whole of England and Wales. They are available from good bookshops like Waterstones and Blackwells, and larger branches of W.H. Smiths, as well as Stanfords in London and Bristol. Stanfords also provide an order and delivery service from their website at www.stanfords.co.uk.

If you plan on doing a bit of sightseeing while you're touring, then some good reads are the Rough Guide volumes for England and Wales (www.roughguides.co.uk). These are also available in a number of language translations.

Finally, some very much underrated sources of local information when you're touring the countryside are the local village stores, post offices and country pubs, especially in the more rural and out-of-the-way places. If you're in desperate need of some special service, or you want to find out more about some local feature, then these are good places to start asking questions.

Fuel

Unleaded petrol is now available at all UK petrol stations. The pumps/nozzles are usually green and the fuel has a 95 octane rating. In the UK look for an ultra low sulphur content fuel (ULS), as due to the complex workings of the British tax system this should be slightly cheaper. A Super Unleaded fuel is also widely available with a 98 octane rating. The old 4-star leaded petrol has now been superseded by the so-called 'lead replacement petrol' or LRP. This uses red pump handles and is often still marked with the four stars, which can be a little misleading. However it may dissapear completely soon as sales continue to fall.

It's still possible to get true leaded 4-star petrol, but the outlets are few and far between. Look for the name Bayford Thrust on the garage forecourt, or visit their website at www.leadedpetrol.co.uk to find the location of their outlets.

Diesel is also available at nearly every petrol station, and if you're visiting from the EU, then you'll be surprised at how expensive it is. But since there aren't any production bikes that run on diesel at the moment, this price difference is largely irrelevant. More to the point is the fact that diesel fuel pumps have either black or blue nozzles, so if you find yourself using one of these to fill your fuel tank, then you're probably just about to make a very expensive mistake!

Going Touring

So what's involved in going touring on your bike in the UK? I'm going to try and answer some if not all of your questions in this section. Everything here is based upon practical experience, sometimes by getting it wrong once and then working out the right way to do it, but also by seeing the results of other people's mistakes.

The Right Bike

The best bike to go touring on is the million-dollar motorbiking question, and you won't be surprised to discover that there's more than one answer. It all depends on who you ask.

Talk to a bike manufacturer or a dealer and it's got to be a fully-dressed tourer with panniers, top box, abs, cruise control, and all the bells and whistles that they can sell you. Very nice if you can afford it and if that's your thing, but for most of us the bike of choice is the one that we currently own; which means that you can go touring on just about anything - from a Pan European to a BSA Bantam - just so long as it's reasonably reliable and you're aware of its limitations. If you're taking a pillion then there's more things to consider, but I have seen people touring two-up on an R6 - that's either dedication or masochism, I'm not sure which! The truth of the matter is that having what someone else believes is the right bike is less important than you having the right frame of mind. I'd personally draw the line at a motocrosser or a stroker, but there are many who'd disagree, and even more who take classic or even vintage bikes on extended trips.

Planning the Trip

First of all you need to have some sort of idea of where you're going, what you're going to do when you get there, and for how long you're going to be away. It doesn't have to be incredibly detailed, but you need some sort of a plan. After all, you don't want to waste valuable time when you get there working out what to do next – you want to get on and do it! At the same time don't plan every hour of the trip, as this won't give you the flexibility to accommodate the unexpected, or to investigate something interesting that you may come across.

You could opt to head for a single destination, make that your base and ride out each day. Or maybe go for a full-blown tour with a new stop each night. Or something in-between. Think carefully about how many miles you can or will even want to ride each and every day. And don't forget to consider the capabilities of the bike that you're riding, and if you're travelling two-up then think about your pillion as well.

If there's a group of you going, do you all have the same riding ability? Having a couple of riders turning up at the hotel four hours after everyone else and just as they're serving the dessert, is not going to go down too well. And if it's your first time in that part of the country, be a little conservative about what you're trying to achieve. Allow time for refreshment and fuel stops and to take a look around. If you find you have time to spare each day, then you can always get out the maps and alter the routes. This is much better and less dangerous than riding 'til you're ready to drop at the end of each day.

Clothing

Once you've worked out where you're going, and for how long, you can start to think about how much clothing and other essentials you need to take with you. First of all there's the daily basics like socks, underwear, toiletries, T-shirts, etc. Then look at the weather you can expect at that time of year to determine warmth and waterproof factors of the other clothes that you'll need when you're not riding. The further north and west you travel in the UK the more likely you are to run into rain, although the British will tell you that you can expect rain any time and anywhere, it's a part of our heritage! More accurately, it's to do with the prevailing southwesterly Atlantic airstream. It's also going to get cooler as you head north. But don't forget that for most of the time you'll be wearing your bike clothing.

Finally, don't forget all those other essentials without which modern man (and woman) cannot survive – mobile phones/chargers, electronic organisers, personal stereo systems – you can make your own lists.

At the end of this exercise you'll probably find that you've assembled a small mountain of clothing and other items that you simply must take (if you have a pillion, it's a mountain range), and there's no way that it will all go on the bike. So what do you do?

- Pack the whole lot into a set of suitcases and go by car. Anyone who believes this is a serious option should stop reading this book immediately.
- Consider purchasing additional luggage for the bike. But if you've already fitted panniers, a top box and a tank bag, and your pillion wears a rucksack, then there's not a lot further you can go here - although a sidecar and a trailer could be an option for some!
- Pack as much as you can, and when you run out of new clothes halfway through the trip, you buy new stuff and throw the old clothes away. You could also get the chauffeur to deliver the luggage to the hotel each night in the Rolls Royce! Seriously though, if you're planning quite a long trip and your luggage and laundry facilities are limited, then this is a possibility especially for things like underwear and socks.
- Shorten the duration of the trip. What! – after you've done all the planning and made all the arrangements? You've got to be joking!
- Be ruthless with what you take. This really is the only option. Hotels, B&Bs and guesthouses are pretty relaxed in their dress standards, and jeans, T-shirt and trainers are not usually a problem; and if you're camping then you can wear what you please. Half a dozen T-shirts, a pair of jeans, another pair a lightweight trousers, shorts, a short-sleeved shirt, a sweatshirt and a fleece can keep you clothed for a couple of weeks with some careful management. You can also wash some 'small' items at overnight stops or find a laundromat in larger towns. Do you really need a complete change of clothes and shoes each evening – and a fresh shirt every day? And do you really want to turn your bike into a two-wheeled removals van? Remember, the object of the trip is to go touring on the bike – not to take part in a mobile fashion show!

But however ruthless you are, you'll nearly always find that you don't wear everything that you take. So you're still taking too much!

At the other extreme you could just take what you can get in your tank bag. However, after a few days travelling, you might find that some establishments refuse you admission!

If you're riding with a pillion, split the luggage capacity 50/50. Do not under any circumstances get into a discussion on this matter.

Finally, don't pack everything to capacity when you set out. Leave some space for those strange little knick-knacks that we all buy at some time or other when we're on holiday.

Other Essentials

As well as clothes, there are a number of other items that you should consider taking with you. Some of them also appear in other sections, but repetition is no bad way of getting a point across.

- Ear plugs. If you don't normally use them on the bike then you should. When you're riding long distances they're essential. Deafness from exposure to high noise levels is cumulative and non-reversible. That's the lecture over.
- Visor cleaning fluid/tissues. The UK's flying insect population springs into life when the sun comes out and appears to be magnetically attracted to helmets. In summer your visor will need frequent cleaning.
- Waterproof winter gloves. It rains in the UK, even at the height of summer. Yes, really!
- Pocket knife/Swiss Army knife/Multi-tool. A thousand and one uses, too numerous to mention. You may never need it, but when you do you'll be glad you bought it with you. And it takes up so little space.
- Small torch such as a mini-Maglite. Useful for reading maps in the dark when you can't find the hotel or campsite at the end of a days ride, as well as looking for that essential item that's just fallen down inside the bike's fairing.
- First Aid kit for minor human body repairs to the cuts and grazes that we all seem to acquire on holiday. It should also have a supply of those little round white tablets that reconnect the body and mind to the environment after a heavy night discussing the day's riding!
- Spare light bulbs for the bike.
- Side stand pad. A small, durable plastic disk that's essential for sportsbike riders with no centre stand when you pull up on gravel parking areas. Why can you never find a flattened Coke can when you want one?
- Puncture repair kit. Obvious really, and much easier than carrying a spare.
- If you're coming to the UK from abroad then you must display a nationality sticker on the bike, or have a 'Euro' number plate fitted. Legally, any vehicle registered in one country that is used on the roads of another country, must display one or other of these at the rear of the vehicle.
- Cargo net. One of the best bike accessories ever invented. Increases the luggage capacity of any bike so that you can bring home those knick-knacks you've bought which won't fit in the panniers, because they're already full of clothes that you haven't worn. Also useful for carrying six-packs back from the supermarket.
- Spare set of bike keys. If you lose or damage your keys when you're a long way from home then you're really stuck. Unless you're very lucky and can get a spare cut locally, then the only alternative may be to have the bike recovered. End of holiday –

game over! If you're travelling with a group of friends, swap the spare keys among the group. Don't ever leave the spares on the bike, and if your bike has hard luggage then don't lock them in the panniers or top box! Sounds obvious, but it's been done before. If you're travelling with a pillion, then give them the spare set. Make sure you also have a spare transmitter for any alarm or immobiliser fitted to the bike, as well as a spare battery for same.

- A can of chain lube. You'll be riding a fair number of miles each day, and the chain and sprockets will get more than the usual amount of grief from the dust and water on the road. Do it religiously at the end of each day's ride and you shouldn't have any problems. Or fit an automatic chain oiler. Or buy a bike with shaft drive!
- A small roll of gaffer or tank tape. Invaluable for providing temporary fixes for a wide variety of motorcycle problems; from repairing cracked body panels, to securing damaged luggage, to holding zips together on clothing. Can also be used to protect the bike's paintwork from abrasion by soft luggage.
- Take along half a dozen cable ties as well and there's nothing you can't do a temporary fix on.
- If you've still got the warranty book for the bike, then there's a useful dealer list in the back that could help if you need emergency help or parts.
- A good disc lock, U-lock, or lightweight cable lock for that added piece of mind.

LUGGAGE

Unless you're going to walk around in your riding clothes all day and every day and not change (Yeech!), you'll need some sort of luggage. Its capacity will really depend on how much you decide to take with you (see *Clothing*) and how long you're going for.

Luggage for motorbikes comes in two types – hard and soft. Which you choose to use will depend on personal preferences and also on the type of bike that you ride. But don't overload the bike. Any luggage that you fit will affect its handling, and the heavier it is and the further away from the bike's centre of gravity, the greater the effect. You can counteract this to some extent by winding up the pre-load on the rear suspension and perhaps stiffening the rear damping.

Check the bike's handbook for any advice from the manufacturer. When the bike's loaded up you'll also find that it's more susceptible to cross winds and air turbulence from other traffic. You may have to adjust your riding style, road speed and positioning to counteract these effects.

Hard Luggage

Considered by some to be the 'Rolls Royce' option for touring, and by others to make a bike look like a delivery van, few would argue that hard luggage is eminently practical. Modern systems are made out of impact-resistant ABS plastics although one manufacturer uses aluminium, and are completely waterproof (Check the rubber seal between the lid and base before use, to make sure that it hasn't been damaged or started to rot – a light smear of Vaseline or similar can work wonders here). The cases attach to mounting

frames that have to be fitted to the bike, but lock in place for added security when parking up for a break or going sightseeing. At the end of a day's riding they unlock quickly and easily, so that you can be showered, changed, and down in the bar while others are still fighting the bungee cords and buckles on their luggage. So if they're that good, why doesn't everyone use them?

- They're only available for certain bikes – the ones that are considered by manufacturers to be 'suitable' for touring.
- They're expensive – a full set of panniers, top box, and the fitting brackets is going to cost around £500-£600.
- The mounting brackets require some basic engineering skills to fit, but you could always pay your dealer to do this work for you.
- Purists will say that all the brackets and boxes spoil the bike's lines, although most systems these days are quite well styled.
- Top boxes are notorious for causing wind turbulence problems that affect a bike's handling. It's much reduced if you carry a pillion, in which case you'll probably need the extra luggage space anyway – and the pillion gets a backrest for free!
- If you change your bike, you'll need to buy and fit a new set of mounting brackets so you can re-use the cases - possibly.

At the end of the day the decision on whether to use hard luggage is a personal one, assuming that it's available for your bike. But if you're planning on doing some serious touring, then it's an option worth considering.

There's one final benefit of hard luggage that none of the manufacturers mention. If you're unfortunate enough to drop the bike, then panniers can prevent an awful lot of damage, both to the bodywork and the bike's mechanical components. Surprisingly, they'll probably only receive a few scuff marks or cracks at the worst, and a replacement will cost a lot less than a new fairing panel and engine covers!

Soft Luggage

This is the universal solution to carting stuff around on your bike. No matter what bike you've got, you should be able to find something to fit it.

Made from a heavyweight Cordura material, usually with a plastic inner coating, there's a variety of equipment available from a number of manufacturers over a range of prices. Generally speaking the more expensive the item, the better will be its build quality and the versatility of its fittings. However, it's always a good idea to take the bike with you when making a purchase, just to make sure that it will fit properly and not mask any of the controls. This is especially so for sportsbikes with high level exhausts. If you're using throwovers they must have plenty of clearance on the silencer(s), otherwise you could end up with a melted and burnt pair of jeans (seen that!)

Although some soft luggage claims to be waterproof, most isn't and will only keep the contents dry in a brief, light shower. Therefore unless you want to turn up in the bar at the end of the day looking as though you've just taken a shower with your clothes on, err on the side of caution and pack everything in waterproof bags before stowing them in the luggage. Heavy-duty plastic bin liners are ideal for this purpose. It's also a good idea to use a separate bag for each type of item that you're taking; T-shirts in one bag, underwear in another, etc., and label them accordingly. This way you don't have to unpack everything just to find a clean pair of socks.

There are four basic types of soft luggage; tank bags, pannier systems, tail packs and rucksacks.

Tank Bags. Considered by most people to be absolutely essential for touring. It should have a clear pocket on top for route instructions, notes, maps, etc., but if you're riding two-up and have a means of communicating with your pillion, you might want to think about using a back-mounted map pocket, and let them do the navigating.

Even if you've got hard luggage on the bike, you'll still find a tank bag useful. Most use magnets to attach the bag to the metal fuel tank, with an auxiliary strap that can be secured around the headstock. On most faired bikes, the magnets alone will hold the bag firmly in place at highly illegal speeds, but on un-faired bikes you'll need the strap as well to stop the bag hitting you in the chest at 90mph before disappearing down the road behind you! You might also want to consider putting a soft cloth or sheet of thin plastic over the tank to prevent the possibility of the bag scratching the paintwork.

If your bike has a plastic tank, then magnets are no good and you'll need a tank bag with a strap system to hold it in place. The French company Baglux do custom tank covers with clips to attach a variety of different shapes and sizes of bag. You can even have the whole lot colour-coded to match the bike's paintwork. Some bike manufacturers who use plastic fuel tanks (BMW, Triumph) produce their own tank bag systems. Talk to your dealer to find out what's available.

You should also check the height of the bag when you're sitting on the bike. Tourers have a more upright riding position and can accommodate a taller tank bag without obscuring the instruments or the road ahead. Sportsbikes by contrast, position the rider over the tank, and if the bag's too tall you may end up with the chin bar of your helmet resting on the top of the bag. If you've ever seen a rider peering over the top of a fully expanded tank bag on a 998 then you'll know what I mean.

Throwover Panniers. These fit over, under, or around the pillion seat of the bike, with a bag hanging down either side. They're held in place with a mixture of Velcro strips, plastic clips, and bungee cords, and offer a wide range of adjustment so that they'll fit almost any bike. There's one system that has a harness that you can leave on the bike, and then clip the bags to it when you want to carry luggage. Make sure that whatever system you choose fits your bike properly before parting with your money, or alternatively have the guarantee of a full refund if there's a fitting problem.

Check the following:

- They mustn't foul any part of the rear suspension at any point in its travel.
- They don't flap around in the breeze
- They can't be pulled off the bike in any direction, as you don't want them disappear-

ing down the road behind you. Be particularly brutal when checking this, but get a friend to hold on to the bike while you're doing it!

- They shouldn't obscure the pillion pegs or make it impossible to carry a passenger. You may be going solo on this trip, but next time it may be different!
- There should be at least one inch (25mm) of clear air between the panniers and any part of the exhaust system when stuffed full (most bags also have a heat reflective layer built into the lower face).

Different pannier systems have different capacities, but don't go straight for the biggest just on the grounds that it will give you more space. To make it fit properly and stay in place securely, soft luggage has to be filled. So if you're using it on a short trip, do you really want to have to fill half of it with newspaper or bits of foam rubber? Some systems offer a variable capacity by using zip-out expansion sections, so are worth considering.

And don't forget to protect any areas of the bike's bodywork that might be rubbed by the throwovers. A couple of strips of gaffer tape on the body panels can work wonders here.

Tail Packs. These used to be small bags that could be bungeed onto the pillion seat or rack, and were more suitable for weekend breaks, but I've also seen a leather suiter strapped to the back of a Fireblade! However, a number of manufacturers are now producing packs with capacities of around 60-90L, which is enough to keep most people supplied with life's essentials for a two-week trip. They come in a variety of designs from tubular sacks to things that look like expanding holdalls, with one type using a rack system that can carry one or two bags that zip together. Most of them use the pillion seat for the main support, which only makes them suitable for solo riders. However, some can be attached to a rack behind the seat, freeing up the pillion space, but you'll need to make sure that you don't overload the rack and its mountings.

Rucksacks. More personal luggage than bike luggage, and they're probably not the best choice for a touring holiday. If you're going to be away for any length of time then capacity is going to be a problem. You're going to need something like a 50-60L backpack, and doing 200+ miles a day with something that size on your back isn't going to be very comfortable or safe. You certainly won't be able to carry a pillion. A small day sack would be a much better proposition, but even something this size can cause pillion problems.

One item of personal luggage that is very useful on a bike is a "bum-bag". You can keep all your money and documents plus other oddments securely on your person at all times, but just make sure that it's got a locking buckle.

Bike Preparation

You've worked out where you're going to go, so you've got a reasonable idea of the mileage you expect to do, and you've got a feel for the load that you'll be carrying on the motorcycle. The next thing is to make sure that the bike will get you all the way there and back safely, in one piece, and without breaking down. This doesn't require an engineering degree, just a reasonable amount of common sense and a methodical approach. Of course, we're assuming before we start that the bike has been serviced regularly, is in good mechanical order, doesn't belch smoke from the exhaust and need a pint of oil every hundred miles, and the engine doesn't rattle like a bucket of nails.

First, it's a good idea to do a visual check on the bike. If everything looks OK and there's nothing about to drop off or fall apart, it's time to start our checklist.

1. When was the bike last serviced? Given the mileage that you expect to cover on the trip and the miles that you'll probably do before you go, will it be well past its next service interval before you get back? If so, then it's a good idea to pop it into your dealer for a good check over. Tell him what you're planning on doing and where you're going and he should be able to come up with a service scheme that will keep you going. Or you can always do the service yourself.
2. Check the condition of the tyres. Is there enough rubber on them to last the trip? If there's any doubt, fit new but keep the old covers. This is much less hassle than trying to get new tyres fitted while you're on your holiday. You can pop the old ones back on later and wear them down to the canvas when you're back home.
3. Give the bearings on the headraces, wheels and swing arm a good going over. Any play or binding should be investigated and corrected before you leave. You don't want the bike wobbling all over the place when you're negotiating a twisty B-road (unless you ride like that anyway!).
4. Check the brake pads and discs, front and rear. They're probably going to get a fair bit of punishment during the trip, so if the pads are more than half worn, get new ones and either fit them before you go or take them with you. Also check the operation of the brakes. If there's any sponginess they should be bled, and if the fluid's more than two years old it's probably a good idea to change it. Replacing the original rubber lines for braided Goodrich or Aeroquip type can rejuvenate your braking system.
5. Check all the control cables (throttle/choke/clutch) for smooth operation. If there's any notchiness or stiffness, then they probably need lubricating. This can be done with something like WD40, or better still use a cable oiler. If the problem persists, then the cable may be damaged and should be replaced before you go. Alternatively, take a spare cable which you could tape in place alongside the existing one to make it easier to fit.
6. Check the condition of the chain and sprockets. If there are any stiff links or the chain has passed its stretch limit or the sprockets are hooked, replace the lot.
7. Check the cooling system. If your bike is air or oil cooled then skip this. There should be no signs of any leaks and the rubber hoses should be in good condition. Any that show surface cracks when you pinch them should be replaced. Also make sure that all hose clips are tight. They can loosen over time as the rubber hose beneath them compresses and hardens.
8. Check the oil level and top up to Max if necessary.
9. Finally, make sure that all fasteners are secure and all the lights are working.

You might want to consider putting together a spares package to take with you. This could include such things as a small 1L can of engine oil, a spark plug, fuses, some electrical tape and any other small items that you consider useful.

And that's about it. The whole thing should only take you a couple of hours at the most.

England On Two Wheels

As the largest country in the United Kingdom, England has a great variety of scenery and roads which make it an ideal venue for touring on two wheels. But size doesn't always bring benefits as it also has the highest population. This means that you get a lot of people squeezed into a fairly small space. Historically, the southeast of the country has always had the most people per square mile, and London and its suburbs and satellites stretches across a large part of the region. But it's not the only city in the country, and the industrialisation of England in the 18th and 19th centuries bought about a big growth in the size of the cities and an influx of people that still continues to this day.

In the 21st century, with more leisure time available to more people, an overall increase in disposable income and the ever increasing car ownership syndrome, the countryside has become the 'great escape' for many, especially at weekends. This, and the commercial growth of the country, has placed more pressures on the road system than ever before, and while there is a very good motorway network that links major centres and carries the bulk of the long-distance traffic, its development and construction has so far been unequal to the growth in car ownership. And anyway, who wants to spend all their time travelling on a three lane dual-carriageway? The challenge for the motorcyclist is how to avoid the busy bits and still get to the good bits. And don't forget that you need to look out for those Gatso things that are popping up everywhere like crocuses after the winter thaw.

Geography

England is very roughly triangular in shape, with the base of the triangle running from the South Foreland in Kent to Land's End in Cornwall, and the apex pointing north at Scotland. The terrain is highest to the north and west, where the rocks are also the oldest, most disturbed and the hardest. The land then gradually falls away to the south and east where the rocks are newer and softer.

In the northwest, the most spectacular feature of the landscape is the area called the Lake District. Here, the ancient volcanic and igneous rocks that intruded through the sandstone strata have been worn away by the glacial action of the last Ice Age to form the wide deep valleys that characterise the area. The melting ice and the subsequent high rainfall caused many of these valleys to flood, giving rise to the numerous lakes in the region. To the east the landscape is gentler, but the fells and high moorland of the border counties of Northumberland and Durham have a desolate beauty about them.

Exmoor

The north of England's other major geographical feature is the Pennines. This chain of Carboniferous rocks and millstone grits runs south from the Cheviot Hills in what has been called the 'Backbone of England', reaching down as far as Staffordshire. The purity and softness of the water that runs out of the grits was one of the main reasons for the growth of the woollen and cotton industries in this area, and the subsequent development of the towns and cities of Leeds, Bradford, Halifax, Huddersfield, and to some extent Manchester. The coal measures and ore-bearing strata that are associated with this area gave rise to major industrial centres, and the whole region became the powerhouse of the Industrial Revolution.

The midland plain, centred around Birmingham, Wolverhampton and Walsall is also a region rich in mineral deposits, as well as having areas whose soil has excellent agricultural properties. It separates the northern hills from the ancient rocks and granites that make up the southwestern peninsular of Cornwall and Devon. The northern coastline of this peninsular along the Bristol Channel is steep and rugged, whilst the southern coastline is much lower and more intimate although no less picturesque. Between the two, a high central plain and the weathering of the granite has resulted in a remote moorland landscape.

Along the south of the country, in an area extending from Dorset through to Kent and north as far as Oxfordshire, a vast chalk sheet provides an undulating, rolling landscape with rounded hills and fertile soils. The limestone formations of the Mendip Ridge south of Bristol and the Cotswolds to the north are a part of this chalky layer, and are separated from the Cornish granites by the flat expanses of the Somerset Levels. To the east another limestone ridge, the Chiltern Hills, runs southwest from Bedfordshire all the way to the Thames at Goring, where it is breached by the river. Beyond this, the chalk ridge is much lower but can still be recognised across Salisbury Plain and into the New Forest. Further east, the land becomes gentler, and in the Fenland areas of East Anglia and around The Wash it assumes an almost billiard table like appearance, with large areas at or below sea level. This is also a rich agricultural region.

In the far south east of the country, the rolling chalk landscape forms the spectacular North and South Downs which face each other across the Kent Weald. The great thickness of the chalk sheet can best be seen in the cliff faces here along the English Channel, and nowhere more so than at Dover and Beachy Head.

Getting There

If you're coming to England from Wales or Scotland, then it's simply a matter of pointing the bike in the appropriate direction along a suitable road. But if you're coming from the other side of any stretch of water, then you'll either need to fit balloon tyres or take a ferry or the tunnel. I'd go for the ferry or tunnel if I was you!

From Ireland there's a good range of ferry services available, details of which are given in the Road Riders Guide to Scotland and Ireland. If you're coming to England from Europe then you'll be using a ferry to cross the English Channel or the North Sea. And there's even one to Scotland!

The table on the next page shows the various ferries and crossings. These were as correct as possible at the time of going to press, but please check before you set out since the ferry companies may well have changed their schedules and services by the time you read this!

Operator	Route	Details	Time	Phone	Website
Brittany Ferries	Santander - Plymouth	Twice weekly	24 hrs	08705 561 600	www.brittany-ferries.com
	Cherbourg - Poole	3 daily	$4^{1}/_{4}$ hrs		
	Roscoff - Plymouth	1- 3 daily	5 hrs		
	St Malo - Portsmouth	Daily	9 hrs		
	Caen - Portsmouth	3 daily	6 hrs		
	Le Havre - Portsmouth	3 daily	6-8 hrs		
Hoverspeed	Calais - Dover	Cat 17 daily	1 hr	0870 240 8070	www.hoverspeed.com
	Dieppe - Newhaven	Cat 3 daily	2 hrs		
		Ferry 2 daily	4 hrs		
P&O Portsmouth	Bilboa - Portsmouth	Twice weekly	29 hrs	0870 2424 999	www.poportsmouth.com
	Cherbourg - Portsmouth	5-7 daily	5-9 hrs		
	Le Havre - Portsmouth	3 daily	6-9 hrs		
P&O Stena Line	Calais - Dover	30 daily	90 mins	0870 600 0600	www.posl.com
P&O North Sea Ferries	Rotterdam - Hull	Daily	11 hrs	08705 202020	www.ponsf.com
	Zeebrugge - Hull	Daily	$11^{1}/_{2}$ hrs		
Seafrance	Calais - Dover	15 daily	90 mins	08705 711 711	www.seafrance.com
EuroTunnel	Calais - Folkestone	4 per hour	35 mins	08703 35 35 35	www.eurotunnel.com
Superfast Ferries	Zeebrugge - Rosyth	Daily	$17^{1}/_{2}$ hrs	0870 234 0870	www.superfast.com
DFDS Seaways	Kristiansand - Newcastle	Twice weekly	16 hrs	08705 333 000	ww.dfdsseaways.co.uk
	Amsterdam - Newcastle	Daily	15 hrs		
	Esbjerg - Harwich	Thrice weekly	16 hrs		
	Cuxhaven - Harwich	Thrice weekly	16 hrs		

What to See

The English countryside is so diverse that it's difficult to know where to start. The south of the country from the Kentish Weald to Land's End at the tip of Cornwall has some cracking scenery, but in the eastern half there are also some of the busiest roads and highest population densities. And if all that wasn't enough there's an inordinate amount of 50mph restricted roads with speed cameras to back them up. Head west and these problems reduce, but keep a look out for the holiday traffic on the main roads in the season. As you head north up into the Midlands there's an increase in the industry and its associated traffic. From the Cotswolds, north along the Welsh border there's plenty of good riding, and East Anglia, although generally as flat as the proverbial pancake, has some excellent roads that sweep through the wide-open panoramas.

For a long time the Pennines has been a playground for the motorcyclist, and while there's excellent riding and magnificent scenery to be had, it's also fallen victim to its own success. Too many accidents and too much speeding has led to the Police being more than aware of what's going on, especially at the weekends.

In Yorkshire the moorland areas offer good riding and scenery, and from here north and west the roads are simply stunning. The Lake District has long been a major attraction for visitors but there are few roads and it has a rainy reputation. East of here, the moors and fells of Northumberland are often ignored by travellers - but this is a mistake.

Accommodation and Information

Tourism is a major industry in England, and as a result there's a tremendous amount of accommodation on offer; from 5-star hotels, to modest B&B establishments, to campsites.

If hotels are your thing, then there's a massive range to choose from. All the big 'chains' are well represented in the cities, towns and commercial areas, but they're geared more towards the business market, the four-wheeled traveller, and the overseas visitor. People on motorbikes are not their forte. There's also an increasing number of so-called 'Country House Hotels' often converted from mansions and other large private residences. All of these places offer all the conveniences you could possibly want - but usually at a price! Private hotels operate slightly lower down the market and can give good value for money.

The English B&B used to be the absolute pits of accommodation - more akin to a wartime concentration camp than somewhere you'd willingly want to stay. But competition from overseas package holidays and an increased awareness from the public has changed all that. B&Bs now offer excellent value for money, with many having almost hotel-like standards. Evening meals are often available and some places even have drinks licences.

There's a classification and inspection system in place throughout the country so that you can be sure of what you're getting, and many have a presence on the internet complete with booking facilities. Almost all are privately owned and range from houses with a spare room to places that exist solely for the tourist market. A lot of farmhouses now offer B&B accommodation to supplement their more traditional income, and the food in these places is usually first class.

In many villages and small towns it's also possible to find accommodation at pubs and inns, and these are also good places to stay. There'll be no problem with getting a drink in the evening and you won't have to bother about riding back to your room - although climbing the stairs can sometimes be a challenge!

There are a number of different publications that provide details on B&B accommodation, but a good place to start is with the tourist boards that cover the areas where you are planning to visit or stay. The table overleaf gives a good selection of internet-based resources for you to start from. A lot of them also offer online booking services, and can also mail you brochures about accommodation and places to visit in the areas that they cover.

A4 at Cherhill

Tourist Board/Information	Website Address
English Tourist Board	www.travelengland.org.uk
English Heritage	www.english-heritage.org.uk
Farm Holidays Bureau	www.farm-holidays.co.uk
South West England	www.westcountrynow.com
South East England	www.southeastengland.uk.com
Heart of England	www.visitheartofengland.com
North West England	www.visitnorthwest.com
Yorkshire	www.yorkshirevisitor.com
The Lake District	www.golakes.co.uk
Northumberland	www.visitnorthumbria.com
London	www.visitlondon.com
Cotswold & Severn	www.visitcotswoldsandsevernvale.gov.uk
Cherwell Valley	www.cherwell-dc.gov.uk
UK B&B Website	www.ukbed.com
Kent Tourist Board	www.kenttourism.co.uk
West Dorset Tourism	www.westdorset.com
Nottinghamshire Tourism	www.nottinghamshiretourism.co.uk
Directory of English Tourist Boards	www.tourist-boards.com/england.htm
Farmhouse Accommodation directory	www.farmhouseaccommodation.co.uk
Pub & Inn Accommodation	www.pub-rooms.co.uk
Pub Accommodation	www.stayinapub.com
UK Accommodation directory	www.smoothhound.co.uk
Hotel, B&B and Inn directory	www.hotelheaven.net
Travelodge	www.travelodge.co.uk
Travel Inns	www.travelinn.co.uk
England campsite directory	www.camp-sites.co.uk

Campsites in England have long been a poor relation of their continental cousins, but things are slowly improving. Whilst there are still site owners whose idea of a suitable pitch is the corner of a ploughed field with a standpipe half a mile away outside the chemical toilet hut, these places are gradually dying out - probably due to cholera, typhoid, dysentery, etc!

As well as the references in the list on the previous page, the following books are useful guides to campsites and camping in England and other UK countries, and can be obtained from most good bookshops.

Title	Publisher	
Alan Rogers' Good Camps Guide: Britain and Ireland	Haynes Publishing	Quality campsites and caravan parks all individually inspected. Lists over 400 sites which are inspected and reviewed regularly. It also has information such as parks for adults only, boat launching, camping for people with disabilities and much more.
Camping and Caravan Parks in Britain	English Tourism Council	The Official guide from the English Tourism Council. Quality assessed camping accommodation in Britain. The listing is in English but instructions on how to use it and useful information are given also in German, Dutch, French and Italian.
AA Caravan and Camping: Britain & Ireland	AA Publishing	Over 1000 sites inspected and given AA pennant ratings. An up-to-date guide to camping establishments in Great Britain and Ireland by the AA. Every campsite is described and graded, contact numbers and websites where available. Photos are given of many establishments.
Camping Sites	IPC Magazines	Top quality sites for tents and motorhomes across the UK. Lists hundreds of sites in England, Wales, Scotland, Northern Ireland and Southern Ireland. Most entries have a star grading, and all include details of location and facilities available.

Roads and Routes

In spite of all the traffic congestion, speed limits, traffic calming schemes, Gatso cameras and other paraphernalia that clutter up the English road system, there are still a surprisingly good number of biking roads spread around the country. What follows in this section are descriptions of some of the routes that I've enjoyed riding.

England is a country of contrasts, so to help you find your way around I've broken it into five arbitrary regions based on geography, and each route has been numbered and assigned to a region. Here's a summary of what you can expect to find in each of them.

South West

This part of the country is noted for it's narrow country lanes, rugged coastlines and cream teas, so progress over the ground is never going to be rapid. It's also one of the UK's prime holiday destinations which means there's always going to be a lot of traffic around. But with more people going abroad and the commendable efforts of the local councils in channelling tourist traffic onto improved trunk roads, there's a lot that's worth exploring on two-wheels. (See routes 1-5)

South & South East

The South-East of England has the highest population density of the country and more vehicles-per-head of the population. There are few if any empty roads, and a lot of speed restrictions that are backed up by cameras. This doesn't sound like ideal biking territory, but there are some good roads around if you take the trouble to find them. Here's a few that I like. (See Routes 6-8)

Midlands

This is 'Heart of England' country, so you can bet your life that there's little chance of getting the road to yourself unless you travel 'out-of-hours' or you're very lucky. But there's some good scenery around, so when progress is delayed there's probably something worth looking at. And there's usually some good places to take a break along the way. (See routes 9-14)

East Anglia

It may have a bit of a reputation for being flat and boring and having few scenic attractions, but there are some good roads out there. (see Routes 15-16)

North

Cumbria and the Lake District are top tourist attractions, it's something to do with all that water, the wide open valleys, and the rugged skyline. Holiday makers and day-trippers flock here in their thousands to experience the tranquillity that's been promoted by the Tourist Authority, and in doing so destroy the very thing that sold them on coming. They also block up the roads and generally get in the way of things, so don't expect any degree of traffic-free riding. In the summer high season and especially at weekends, you really ought to be somewhere else. Over on the East side it's the home of open moorland, mountainous fells, and roads that weave and undulate across the landscape; there's no shortage of scenery in this part of the country. But the roads and the views aren't a well kept secret so you'll also find convoys of coaches, and small towns and villages disappearing under a tourist invasion. (See routes 17-25)

B6277 AT BURNHOPE SEAT (SEE ROUTE 19)

A6 NORTH OF KENDAL (SEE ROUTE 21)

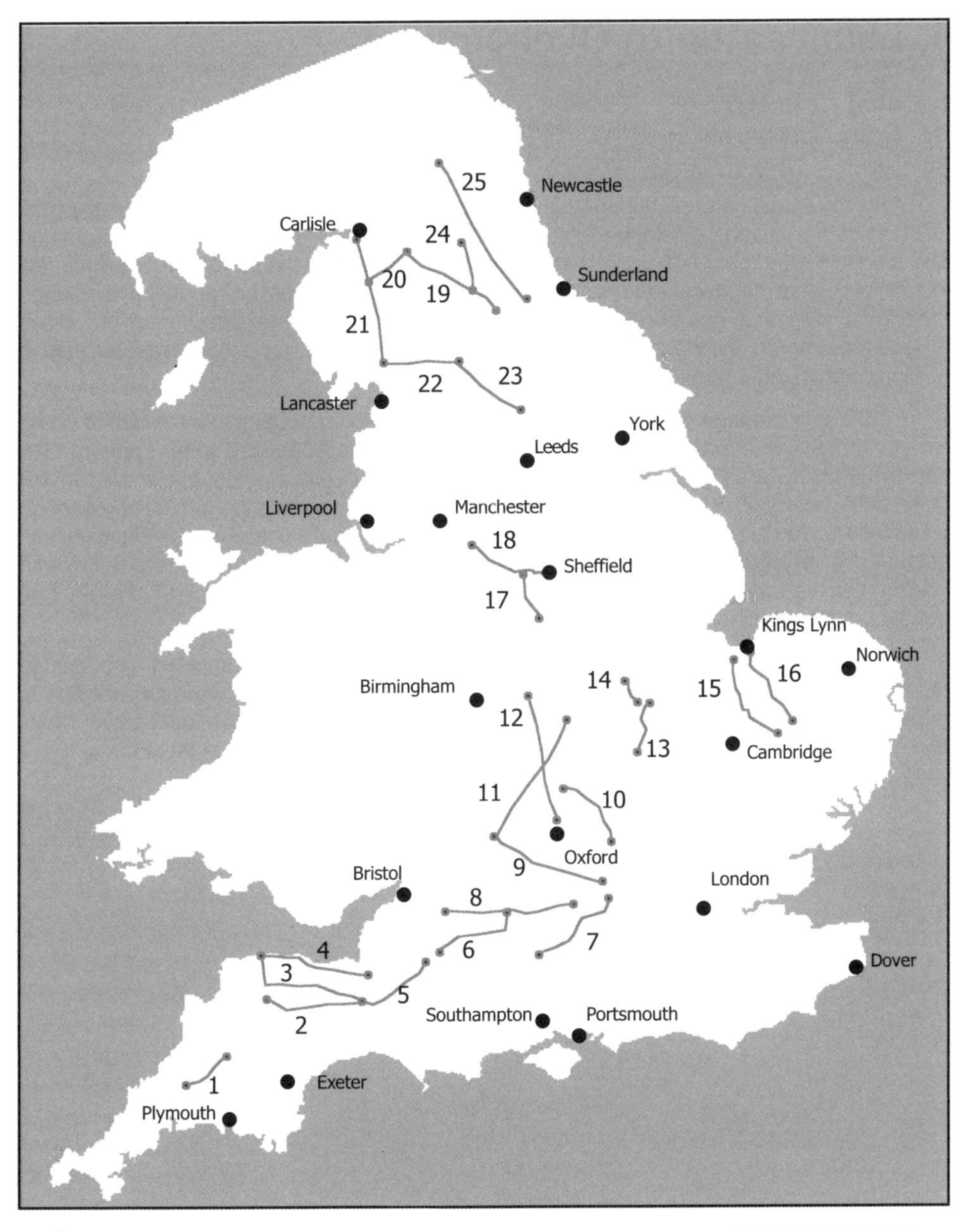

ENGLAND SHOWING APPROXIMATE LOCATIONS OF MAJOR TOWNS AND THE ROUTES IN THIS GUIDE

1. Launceston to Okehampton

Distance: 18 Miles
Surface: Excellent
Scenery: Open Country

Strictly speaking the 'meat' of this route runs from Lifton to the east of Launceston, to just outside the village of Meldon which is a few miles west of Okehampton. Not so long ago this used to be the main A30 trunk road, but the powers-that-be then decided to build a new section of dual-carriageway road just to the north of the old road, call this the A30 and consign the original road to un-numbered oblivion. Good for them I say, as they've given us 11$^1/_2$ miles of deserted, smooth, wide tarmac that sweeps and climbs and dips in the closest approximation of Nirvana that you're likely to find for a long time.

To take advantage of this stroke of road-building good fortune, leave the centre of the old market town of Launceston and head south towards the A30 and Exeter. Then turn left onto the A388 towards Lifton. Follow this road to the junction with the A30, but where the rest of the traffic heads off onto the dual-carriageway, you should continue straight on and through Lifton village. You're now on the old main road, and if you're really unlucky then you might see another two vehicles before the road rejoins the A30 around 11 miles further on. But even if you do, the road is so wide and the view ahead so good that you shouldn't have any real trouble getting past them. Just enjoy the ride.

Back on the A30, at Meldon take the B3260 and head into Okehampton if you need to refuel body and bike. Or just turn round and ride all the way back again to Launceston to refuel and grab some refreshments. There's some good cafes and pubs for a drink or two, and a really superb Fish 'n' Chip Restaurant if you need something a little more filling.

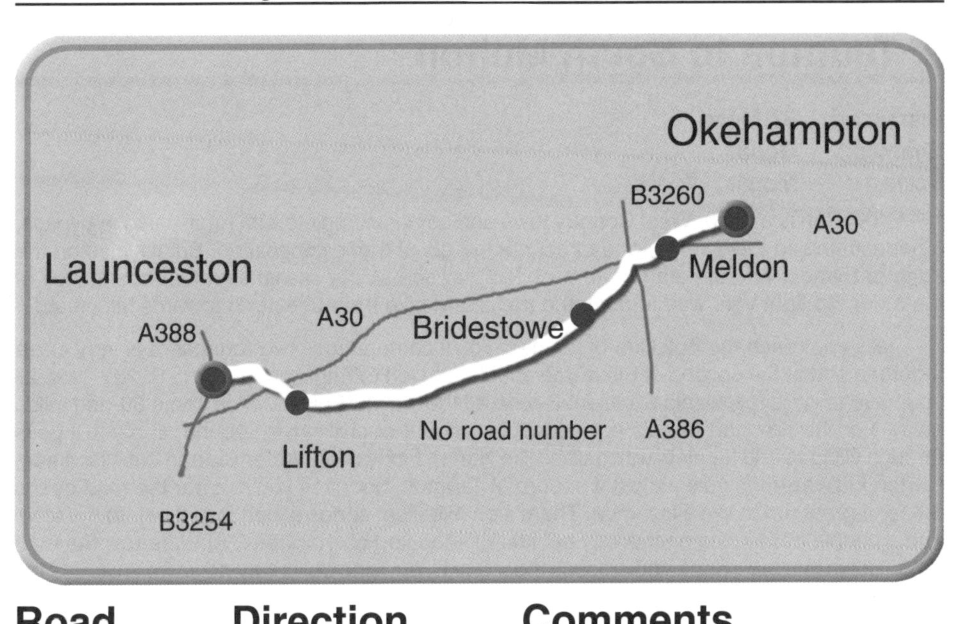

Road	Direction	Comments
	Lifton and A30	Leave town centre
A388	Turn left to Lifton	
A388	To A30	Straight on to Lifton Through village and you are on the old road
No Number	Bridestowe	Continue straight on to the A30 junction
A30	Okehampton	Turn left at Meldon
B3260	Okehampton	Cafes and fuel at Okehampton

2. Taunton to South Molton

Distance: **37 Miles**
Surface: **Good**
Scenery: **Moors, Woods**

Taunton is a major West Country town and comes complete with retail parks, a bypass, a pedestrianised town centre and of course the usual traffic congestion. But it's also on the edge of Exmoor and the start of an excellent run across the scenic southern boundaries of the moor. So fight your way through the traffic and take the A358 north towards Minehead.

As you reach the outskirts of Taunton you'll come across two roundabouts very close together, and at the second of these you should turn left (straight on) onto the B3227. Now all you have to do is follow this excellent B-road all the way to South Molton some 30-odd miles away. For the first part there's a reasonable amount of civilisation around, and you'll pass through villages and hamlets with names like Norton Fitzwarren, Waterrow and Wiveliscombe. Norton Fitzwarren is now almost a suburb of Taunton, but once you're clear the road opens out for a great run to Wiveliscombe. There's an excellent series of bends just before the town and a couple of hairpins on the way out just to keep you on your toes. At Waterrow the road drops down into the village and crosses the infant River Tone on its way down from Clatworthy Reservoir in the Brendon Hills.

Approaching Wiveliscombe

The road now enters Devon, although the only difference this appears to make is that the hedges seem to get a little higher and the road gets a little narrower. Bampton is a good place to take a break as there's a very useful set of public toilets next to the large carpark, and a good selection of pubs for a bit of refreshment.

Leaving Bampton, the road descends rapidly to the River Axe valley where there's an interesting junction as the road crosses the A396; but basically you carry straight on. The Black Cat Garage on the left here looks as though it's stuck in a 1930's time warp!

The B3227 now swings right and climbs out the other side of the Axe valley parallel to the river, and then turns left to head off to the west, following the southern boundary of Exmoor National Park. Hold onto your helmet as this is a truly excellent piece of road that climbs all the way up to Combeswell Gate and then drops down towards the A361. Carry straight on at the small roundabout and pass underneath the trunk road to the T-junction a third of a mile further on. There's a useful petrol station just on the corner. Turn left here and head up the A361 to the next roundabout and then take the first exit back onto the B3227. South Molton is just over two miles further on, and the small town has a good selection of pubs and cafes to offer you refreshment at the end of your journey.

Bampton Church

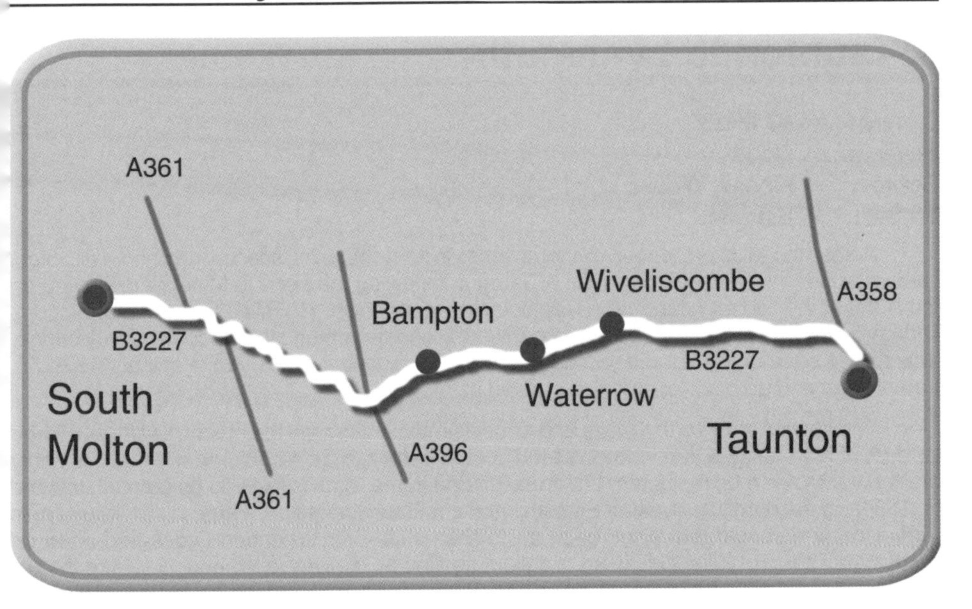

Road	Direction	Comments
A358	Follow Minehead	At outskirts of Taunton take the B3227 at the second of two roundabouts
B3227	Wiveliscombe, Bampton	Follow the road
B3227	South Molton	Straight on at junction with the A396
A361	South Molton	Straight on at small roundabout and join the A361 to the next roundabout
B3227	South Molton	First exit from roundabout onto the B3227 to South Molton where you will find refreshments

3. Taunton to Lynmouth

Distance: 43 Miles
Surface: Good
Scenery: Moors, Woods
To See: Exmoor

Across the wilds of Exmoor, this route takes in some stunning scenery and some excellent Devonian B-roads, so head north out of Taunton following the signs to Minehead, staying on the A358 at the two roundabouts on the outskirts of the town. 1½ miles further on at Bishops Lydeard, turn left onto the B3224 towards Elworthy and go immediately under a railway bridge. This turn is easy to miss and if you go under a railway bridge while you're still on the A358, turn around and go back 'cos you've passed it!

The section to Elworthy twists and turns as it climbs up onto the moors, but it's bordered by a lot of high hedges that in true West Country fashion, hide hard stone walls. So not only are the views are a bit restricted, but any variation in the route is likely to be painful! Join the B3188 from the right just south of Elworthy and continue straight on. Three-quarters of a mile further on you should turn right, back on to the B3224 for Wheddon Cross and head off across the Brendon Hills. This is an excellent section all the way to Wheddon, where there's a tricky crossroads in the centre of the village. Views to the right and the left are very restricted so be extremely careful as you make your way across, staying on the B3224 towards Simonsbath.

At Exford the road drops down to cross the River Exe in the centre of the village, and then continues as the B3223 across Exmoor to Simonsbath. There's a steep downhill approach into the village, and the road does a sharp left-right across the bridge and then climbs away to the left as it heads for the north Devon coast. The road runs in and out of Exmoor Forest all the way to the small village of Simonsbath, where it swings north and heads out into Exmoor proper. The scenery here is wild and barren but under sunny blue skies it's a place of great beauty. The cattle grid across the road as you head out onto the moor is a good reminder to keep an eye open for sheep and other animals, some of which have really suicidal tendencies. And there's a second grid as you head off the moor just around a blind left-hander, so be very careful if the road is damp.

The road descends steeply off the moor and takes in a couple of tight hairpins to drop down into the valley of the Farley Water at Hillsford Bridge where it meets the A39 on the apex of a hairpin. Bear right here and follow the road past Watersmeet all the way into Lynmouth. Turn right here and then immediately left just before the bridge. If you're lucky you'll find somewhere to park in the road (2 hours max - free), but you may have to continue on to the big car park where you'll have to pay.

Exford Village

There's a good display in the town about the 1952 flood which destroyed nearly 100 houses, 28 bridges and took 31 lives.

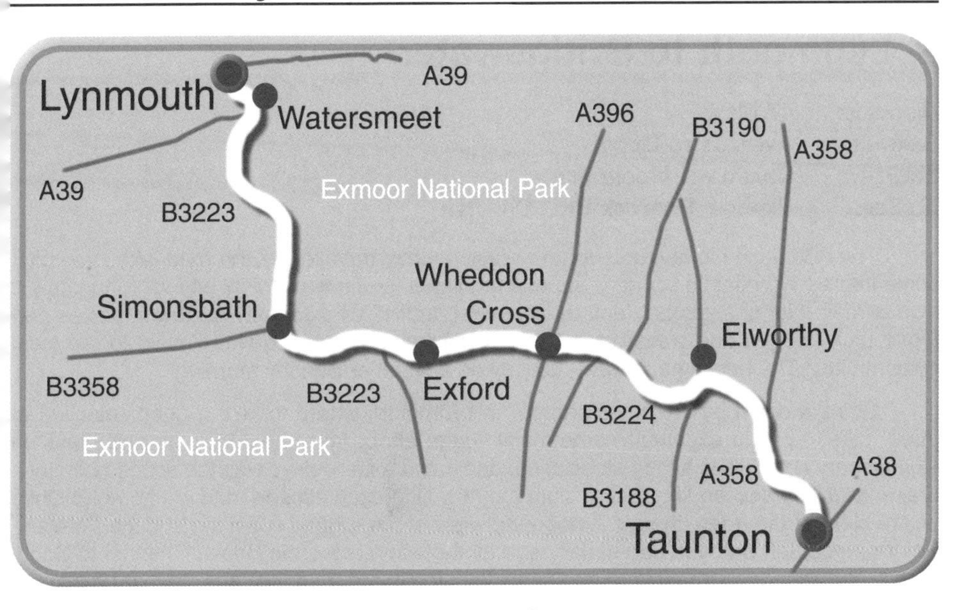

Road	Direction	Comments
A358	Minehead	Turn left on the B3224
B3224	Elworthy	Under bridge
B3224	Wheddon Cross	Join the B3188 from right Turn right back onto the B3224 after 3/4 mile
B3224	Exford, Simonsbath	
B3223	Simonsbath	Petrol at Exford Outside Exford road becomes the B3223
B3223	Lynmouth	Meets the A39. Turn right
A39	Lynmouth	Turn right and immediately left before bridge. Park here or at car park at the end

4. Lynmouth to Bridgewater

DISTANCE: **47 MILES**
SURFACE: **AVERAGE TO GOOD**
SCENERY: **COASTLINE, MOORLAND**
TO SEE: **EXMOOR, PORLOCK HILL, DUNSTER**

The A39 is an old favourite for the West Country traveller, as the road takes you past some impressive coastal scenery, serious gradients, and lots of twisty bits. Unfortunately it also carries a lot of seasonal (and un-seasonal) traffic, it's extremely narrow in places and those high hedges and walls restrict the forward views. It's also well known to the local constabulary. The best time to travel is early on a summer Sunday morning.

Starting down by the small harbour in Lynmouth, where there's a good selection of pubs, cafes and an excellent home-made fudge shop, take the A39 east and head up Countisbury Hill. This is a long steep climb and in the "olden" days was the scene of many a brake failure by descending traffic - note the now little-used escape road on the right. Once you're clear of the trees, there's a wonderful view of the rugged coastline and the Foreland Point on your left and you can usually see all the way across the Bristol Channel to South Wales. But keep a sharp lookout for sheep sleeping in the road, just around that next bend! Past the hamlet of Countisbury (useful pub), the road passes from Devon to Somerset at County Gate and winds across the northern fringe of Exmoor. It then starts a gradual descent, but it's going to get a lot steeper as we're heading for Porlock with its infamous 1 in 4 hill with two hairpins. It used to be a real test of engines (and brakes) as recently as the 1960's. Porlock village is at the bottom and the road is extremely narrow there. In summer it gets very congested.

Stay on the A39, through the one-way system with its climbing hairpin right, and head towards Bridgewater. From here to Minehead the road is fairly good, but it's twisty and the hedges are high. The road runs around the back of Minehead, but it you want to take a break for a walk along the seafront or the amusement park at Pontins, turn left and head for the Town Centre. Past Minehead and with the Brendon Hills on your right, there's traffic lights at a crossroads where you can turn right to visit Dunster and its castle.

The road widens out now and the curves are more open, but there's still some tight and narrow bits to keep you on your toes, so don't get too carried away. Past Watchet and the land begins to flatten as we leave the hills of Exmoor behind and head towards the Somerset Levels. But the road still can't do straight lines so there's no shortage of bends to keep you happy, unless you're stuck behind a convoy of caravans! Bridgewater's the major market town in north Somerset so there's no shortage of services and the traffic that comes with them. Industrial and commercial development has left little of the original town intact, so why not refuel and ride that cracking road all the way back to Lynmouth and the fudge shop!

LYNMOUTH HARBOUR

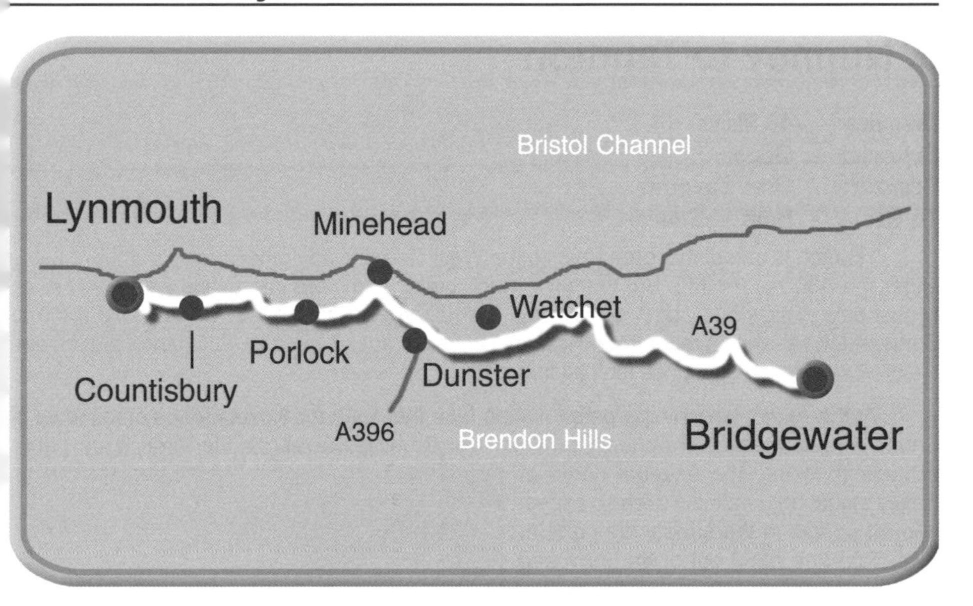

Road	Direction	Comments
A39	Porlock	Take the A39 East up Countisbury Hill
A39	Porlock	1 in 4 hill with sharp bends entering Porlock
A39	Minehead	At Minehead turn left to go to the seafront or carry straight on for Bridgewater
A39	Bridgewater	Turn right at traffic lights just outside Minehead for Dunster Castle
A39	Bridgewater	Services at Bridgewater

5. Nunney to Taunton

DISTANCE: **40 MILES**
SURFACE: **GOOD**
SCENERY: **OPEN COUNTRY**
TO SEE: **BRUTON CHURCH**

Taunton is one of the 'gateways' to the West Country, and most people get there using either the A303 or the M5. But there's a much better and more interesting way if you're on two-wheels. This route starts at Nunney, a small village on the A361 south of Frome in Somerset. It has little to recommend it scenically, but it does have a 24-hour petrol station and a Little Chef, which I suppose isn't all that bad!

At the roundabout by the petrol station take the A359 for 8 miles to the small town of Bruton and its magnificent church on the River Brue. However, it's the three large public schools (one has the unusual name of Sexey's) that dominate the area so expect a lot of people in the streets during term time. Take the A359 out of the town and back into the rolling countryside then follow the signs to Sparkford until you reach the junction with the A371. Turn right here towards Shepton Mallet and pass round the edge of Castle Cary with its one-way traffic light system, and then on to Ansford where you need to turn left to Somerton on the B3153 immediately after crossing the railway bridge. The next 10 miles are a mixture of open countryside and small villages, with only the traffic lights at the A37 crossroads in Lydford getting in the way of things.

A359 NEAR BRUTON

The centre of Somerton has been by-passed to some extent, so the route keeps you away from the town but there's a free car park on the left if you need to stop for anything. From here it's just four not particularly interesting miles to Langport on the banks of the River Parrett. Head down straight through the town and pick up the A378 to Taunton which takes you over the river bridge, up the other side of the valley, on through Curry Rivel, and over the Blackdown Hills to the junction with the A358. Turn right onto this busy road and follow it down to the junction with the M5, but take care as there's a usually active Gatso camera just past Thorn Falcon.

Just before you reach the M5 roundabout there's a lay-by on the right with a 24-hour burger bar that does a mean bacon sarnie, and on the roundabout itself there's an all-night petrol station.

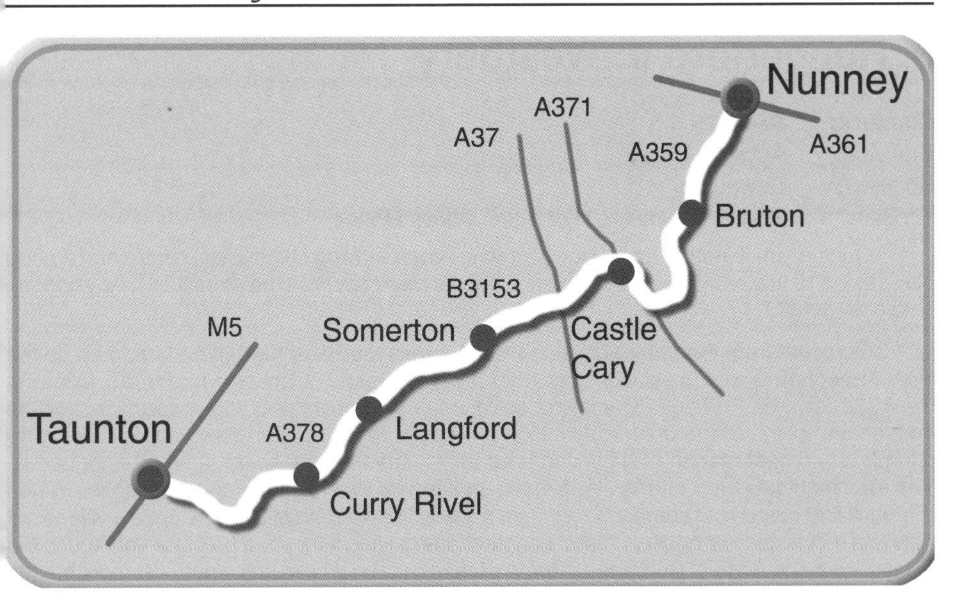

Road	Directions	Comments
A359	Bruton	Good Church
A359	follow Sparkford	Right at junction with the A371
A371	follow Shepton Mallett	Around Castle Cary to Ansford. Left for Somerton after bridge on the B3153
B3153	Somerton, Langford	At Langford pick up the A378 to Taunton
A378	Taunton	Through Curry Rivel to junction with A358
A358	Taunton	

6. Hungerford to Westbury

DISTANCE: 36 MILES
SURFACE: AVERAGE/GOOD
SCENERY: DOWNLAND
TO SEE: WILTON WINDMILL, WESTBURY WHITE HORSE

Once a small market town, Hungerford is now a thriving commercial centre and a good place to visit if you're interested in 'objets d'art', as there seems to be almost as many antique shops as pubs!

Go south from the roundabout on the A4, cross the River Kennet and head on up the High Street taking care to avoid the cars that reverse straight out into the main road, following the A338 towards Burbage. The town centre is fairly compact and you're soon clear of the houses and out onto the open road which sweeps across the open downs before dropping sharply down past Marten and braking hard for a series of very sharp right-left-right bends. The road then gets back into its stride again, making for West Grafton and passing the Wilton Windmill that stands out sharply on the right horizon. Beyond West Grafton, once a village but now just a collection of houses, there's another sharp kink in the road before a final run to the junction with the A346 at Burbage. There's a big roundabout here and a petrol station, but the route takes you straight across and on to the B3087 for Pewsey.

At the T-junction in the centre of Pewsey, turn left on to the A345 Devizes road and follow this around the town and back out into the country. A short run brings you to a roundabout and the Woodbridge Inn on the right. Carry straight on into the village of Rushall, follow the road round to the left and then take the right turn onto the A342 towards Devizes and into the open spaces of the Vale of Pewsey. After Chirton look out for the B3098 turn off to the left and head off down through the village of Urchfont, and then on to Market Lavington. The road is mostly open and clear as it sweeps across the downland towards Westbury. However be careful around Erlestoke, and not just for inmates escaping from the nearby prison. There are a couple of narrow twisty sections here where the road runs between high wooded earth banks, everything gets a bit gloomy, and it's difficult to see oncoming traffic even when they're completely filling the road!

Past Bratton there's a final sweeping open section before Westbury, and the cement works appears on the right like a blot on the landscape. Much more interesting is the Westbury White Horse, and there's a car park on the right just before you enter the town where you can get a good view of it. The current white horse is one of a number dotting the hills in this area and dates from the 18th Century, although it covers the site of an earlier horse that is believed to go back thousands of years, perhaps to the days of the hill fort encampment whose remains are still visible.

WESTBURY WHITE HORSE

Another mile down the road brings you into Westbury, a petrol station and refreshments. Until the 1960's Westbury had been a centre of the wool industry for six centuries, due largely to the good supplies of clear spring water in the area. It also had a large tanning and glove making industry, but the arrival of the railway in the middle of the 19th Century transformed into a rail town.

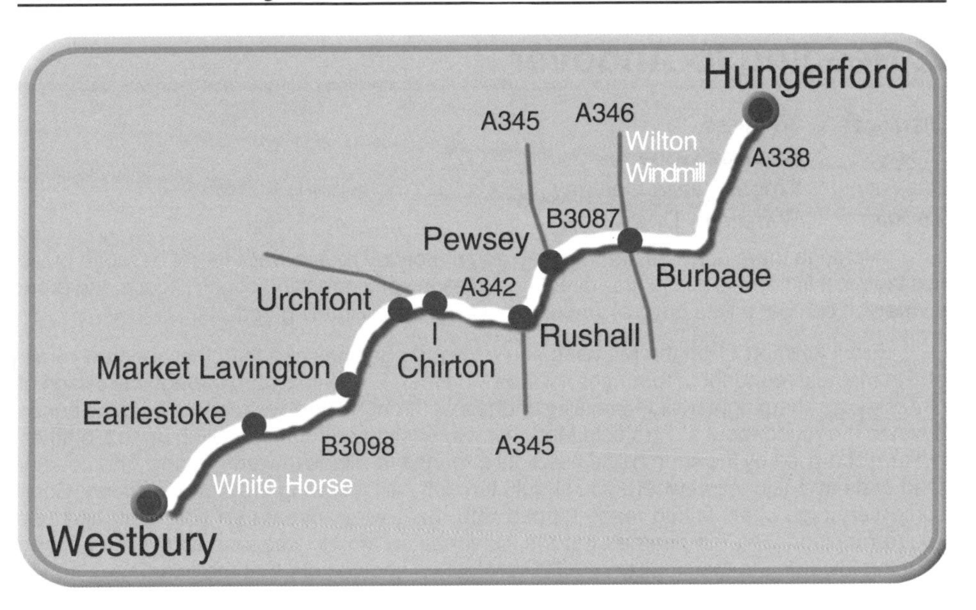

Road	Direction	Comments
A338	Burbage	South from the A4 along the High Street
B3087	Pewsey	Straight on at the roundabout. Petrol station
A345	Follow Devizes	Turn left at Pewsey
A345	Rushall	Turn right here onto the A342
A342	Follow Devizes	Turn left after Chirton onto the B3098
B3098	Westbury	White Horse just before Westbury

7. Reading to Andover

Distance: **33 Miles**
Surface: **Average/Good**
Scenery: **Woods, Open Country**
To See: **Watership Down**

Although there are dual carriageway and motorway routes ways to get between these two towns, this route is a little less direct but takes in some cracking country roads and great scenery. It can get a little busy at times, especially at the Reading end.

From junction 11 on the M4 head south towards Basingstoke for a few hundred yards, and at the next roundabout turn right towards Mortimer. Follow this road through the village of Grazeley, go sharp right over the railway bridge and through some wonderful sweeping bends down to the roundabout at Stratfield Mortimer. Go straight on here and climb up to Mortimer, but turn sharp left by the church and head out through the village towards Tadley. This country road ends at a T-junction where you should turn left, still following the signs to Tadley. Soon some very high chain linked fence topped with razor wire appears on you right, because you're running along the perimeter of the Aldermaston atomic weapons establishment and heading towards the main entrance. CND protesters should note that the guards are armed and their weapons are loaded with live ammunition. This section can get a bit busy in the rush hours, but you won't find 20,000 walkers heading towards Westminster any more at Easter.

There's a big triangular-shaped one-way system on the outskirts of Tadley where you have to turn left, but then you should take the next right and then go straight on, following the boundary of the weapons factory. At the next roundabout go straight on, taking the B3051 to Kingsclere. This road is dead straight for about a mile, but resist the temptation to wind it on. There are three reasons for this; the first part of the road still has a speed restriction on it; it's not uncommon for large animals to leap out of the woods on either side of the road; and there's a garden centre halfway down which seems to attract cloth-capped Volvo drivers like moths around a flame.

Clear of the gardening paradise, this is a great section of road with some challenging bends, some of them a little tighter than you might think at first! Also, keep a look out for gravel on the edge of the road, especially after rain. Finally the road descends to cross the A339 dual carriageway and takes you into Kingsclere. In the centre of the village turn left just before the church, staying on the B3051 and heading towards Overton and Whitchurch. The road climbs steeply to the crest of Watership Down, so look out for colonies of fluffy bunnies. As you drop down the other side, carry straight on where the road to Overton branches off to the left. From here to Whitchurch it's another cracking run with lots of challenging corners and fast straights as the road runs across the downs. The fun terminates (briefly) at a deceptively angled T-junction that's difficult to spot at the end of a fast section of road, so if you're not on the ball you may have to test your stopping power to the limit. Go left at this junction and follow this road down to the roundabout in the centre of Whitchurch. Follow the B3400 here towards Andover, past the petrol station on the left, the church on the right and under the bridge that carries the A34. This last section is quite narrow in places as it twists its way through Hurstbourne Priors and then makes a bee-line towards Andover.

The road ends at a roundabout where it meets the Andover ring road. Turn right here to head around the north side of the town and pick up routes to the town centre, or go left to connect to the A303. If you go this way, then the sliproad onto the westbound carriageway is a real corker!

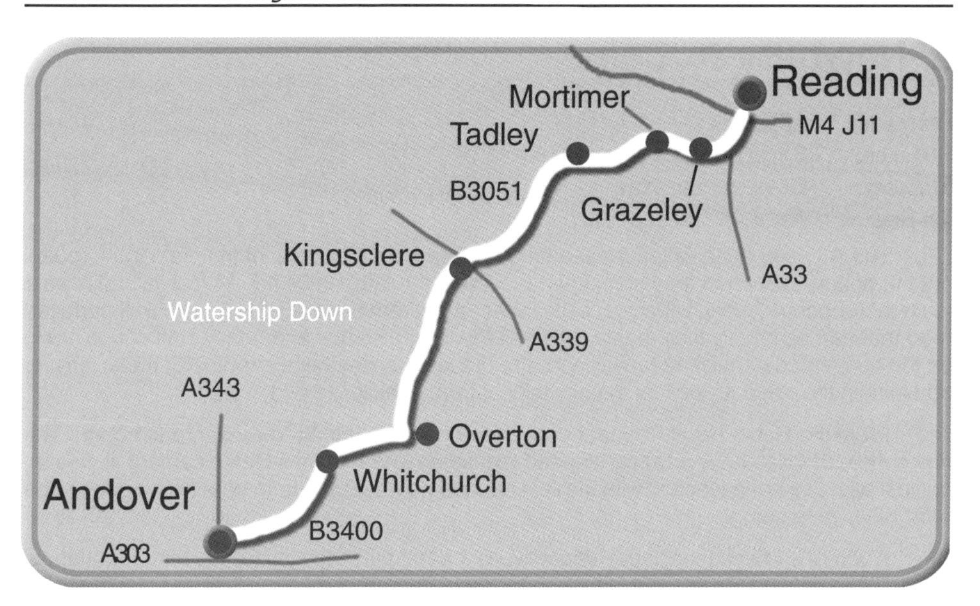

Road	Direction	Comment
A33	Basingstoke	Turn right at the roundabout after 400 yards
Unmarked	Mortimer	Through Grazeley, right over the bridge to the roundabout. Straight on for Mortimer
Unmarked	Silchester Aldermaston	Left at church in Mortimer
Unmarked	Tadley Silchester	Left at T-junction. Aldermaston on your right
B3051	Kingsclere	Cross the A339
B3051	Whitchurch	Left in centre of Kingsclere
B3051	Whitchurch	Left at T-junction
B3400	Andover	Under the A34 to roundabout. Left for the A303, right for town centre

8. Newbury to Calne

DISTANCE: 33 MILES
SURFACE: EXCELLENT
SCENERY: DOWNS, FORESTRY
TO SEE: AVEBURY, SILBURY HILL

The A4 used to be called the Great West Road, and was one of the main trunk routes out of London. But when they completed the M4 in the late 1960s the A4 lost its status as a main thoroughfare, along with most of its traffic. What remains is a wide, quick, well-surfaced road that carries mostly local traffic, while all the long-distance and heavy stuff chugs along on the congested parallel motorway. Great! - but keep a weather eye open for traffic leaving and joining the road, as well as the occasional farm vehicle.

From the Robin Hood Roundabout in Newbury take the A4 towards Marlborough. The first couple of miles have a 30 mph speed restriction and there's a Gatso camera in Speen, but just past this is the junction with the A34 Newbury bypass and from here to Hungerford the road really gets going.

If you're into antiques then Hungerford is a good place to stop (at the third roundabout turn left for the High Street), but if the riding's more important then go straight on at the three mini-roundabouts and stick to the A4. There are also two petrol stations here if you're getting low on fuel. Climbing out of the Kennet valley, the road crests the rise and sweeps left onto a straight section that's proven popular for speed checks.

At Froxfield there's a pub at the start of a 50 mph limit through the village, which ends with a sharp right-hander, and then it's back to normality and another excellent run across the downs and the descent through Savernake Forest into Marlborough. This is a very old, quaint and busy English market town with a characteristic wide main street. On market days it's chaotic, and at other times you need to be very careful as there are two rows of parked cars down the middle of the road and pedestrians everywhere!

Assuming that you've managed to negotiate this meleé, go right at the small roundabout at the end of the High Street and then bear left on the A4 past Marlborough College. Past Fyfield and West Kennet, the ancient Long Barrow burial site is a short walk across the fields to the left, and then the enigmatic mound of Silbury Hill appears ahead. The road runs close to the base of this strange earthwork, and there's a car park just past it on the right where you can take a break and see if you can work out who built it, and why. At the next roundabout carry straight on for the A4 to Calne, but if all these strange Neolithic sites have gotten to you then turn right for the two mile run up to Avebury. Here, the circle of stone monoliths are yet another puzzling piece of our ancient history.

SILBURY HILL AT WEST KENNET

The final stretch of the A4 is wide and open, climbing over the edge of the downs and past the site of Oldbury Castle and the White Horse before dropping down through Cherhill and into Calne. There are plenty of facilities in the town.

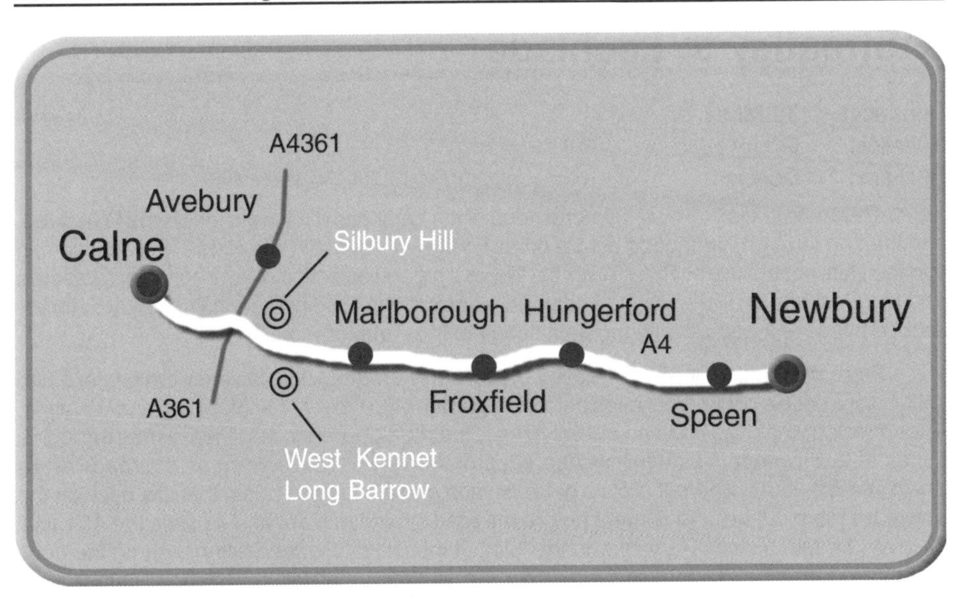

Road	Directions	Comments
A4	Hungerford, Marlborough	Gatso camera at Speen
A4	Hungerford	Turn left for antique shops in town centre, or straight on for Marlborough
A4	Marlborough	Right at end of the High St in Marlborough
A4	Calne	Note West Kennet Long Barrow on left, Silbury Hill on right. Turn right at the roundabout onto the A4361 to visit Avebury, or straight on to Calne

9. Streatley to Lechlade

DISTANCE: 30 MILES
SURFACE: GOOD
SCENERY: DOWNS

This route takes you over the north edge of the Lambourn Downs to the town of Wantage, and then on through Farringdon before crossing the Vale of the White Horse and descending into the valley of the upper River Thames. There's a good selection of tight corners, sweepers and long fast blasts all the way to Lechlade, although the road can get a little busy at times. And Lechlade is a popular day trip destination in the summer months.

From the traffic lights at Streatley, head north on the A329 towards Wallingford and Oxford for a couple of hundred yards before turning left onto the A417 to Blewbury and Wantage. After passing what was once an old toll house, the road descends and then climbs through a series of fast sweepers as it follows the edge of the Downs. Slow down as the roads drops down into Blewbury, where there's a petrol station and a couple of pubs, then it's back on the power for more curves and corners before the road straightens out and crosses the A34 on a new(ish) bridge, passes Harwell with the 'blot' of the Didcot Power Station over on the right, and arrives at the junction with the A4185. Go straight on at this roundabout, through the 'Hendreds' and the 'Lockinges' and into Wantage. Take the ring road system around to the right of the town to avoid the extremely narrow and congested streets in the town centre, following the A417 for Farringdon. The small village of Grove, home of the Williams F1 race team, is a mile or so up the road from here.

Once clear of Wantage and the 'Challows', the road gets going again, across the Vale of the White Horse to a roundabout on the A420. Turn left here, and after half a mile go right at the next roundabout back onto the A417, past the petrol station and into Farringdon. The road skirts the edge of this small town, but if you need any services, then turn right at either of the two roundabouts. Stay on the A417 for a fast run from here to Lechlade with quick corners and good open stretches all the way to Buscot, where there's a sharp right turn to cross a narrow bridge over the River Thames. It you don't want to travel the last mile or so into Lechlade, the Trout Inn on the north side of the bridge makes an excellent stopover, although it gets extremely busy in the summer.

At Lechlade the road ends at a T-junction; turn left here for the village centre, cafes, pubs and the River Thames, or turn right for $^{1}/_{2}$ mile if you need fuel.

THE A417 NEAR BLEWBURY

THE A417 NEAR FARRINGDON

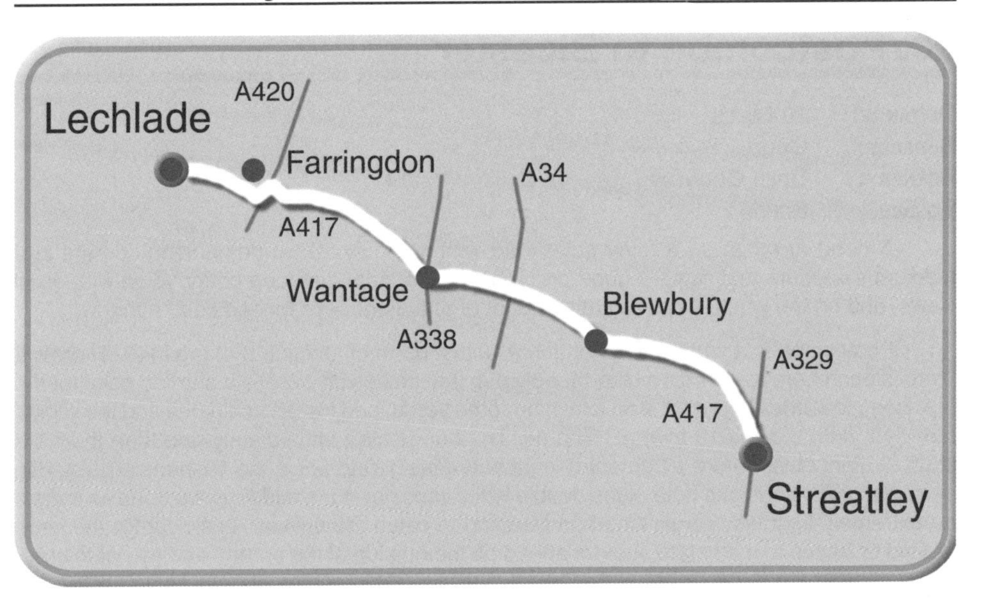

Road	Direction	Comments
A329	Wallingford	Left after 200 yards
A417	Blewbury, Wantage	Through Blewbury, over the A34 and straight on at roundabout to Wantage
A417	Farringdon	Follow ring the road round Wantage and on to the roundabout on the A420
A420	Farringdon	Turn left at the A420, then right back onto the A417 to Farringdon
A417	Lechlade	Through Farringdon and on to Lechlade

10. Postcombe to Bicester

DISTANCE: **20 MILES**
SURFACE: **GOOD**
SCENERY: **OPEN COUNTRY**
TO SEE: **BENDS**

A good run this, on a fairly quiet road with some excellent demanding corners and medium sweepers that require good precision. The scenery is open countryside with good views, and on the whole it doesn't attract a lot of attention. Let's try and keep it that way.

Postcombe is a small village on the A40 just north of junction 6 of the M40. There's a petrol station here as well as a bike-friendly pub that makes an excellent starting point for the trip. Head towards Oxford for a couple of hundred yards, and just as you're leaving the village turn right onto the B4012 towards Thame. The bends start immediately and then there's a short straight blast before a tightening right and a fast left to settle the suspension. You can gas it out of here but take note of the double white lines down the middle of the road as there's an extremely tight left hander up ahead waiting to catch the unwary. Look out for the large arched entrance to the estate straight ahead on the outside of the corner, and try not to use it as an escape road! Two more sharp bends and the 30mph signs appear as you reach the outskirts of Thame.

Turn right here, following the "Through Traffic" signs that allow you to avoid the congestion of the town centre and its speed bumps. Carry straight on across the first two roundabouts and at the third one, take the third exit and follow the signs to Long Crendon, Bicester and the B4011. There's a service area on the right here where you can get petrol and refreshments.

There's a short straight run the village of Long Crendon and its thatched cottages, but keep a look out for the speed humps, and then it's back to open fields and the sweeps up through Oakley and around Brill with it's windmill perched on the hill. Then it's bends all the way to the junction with the A41 where you turn left for the final mile blast into Bicester.

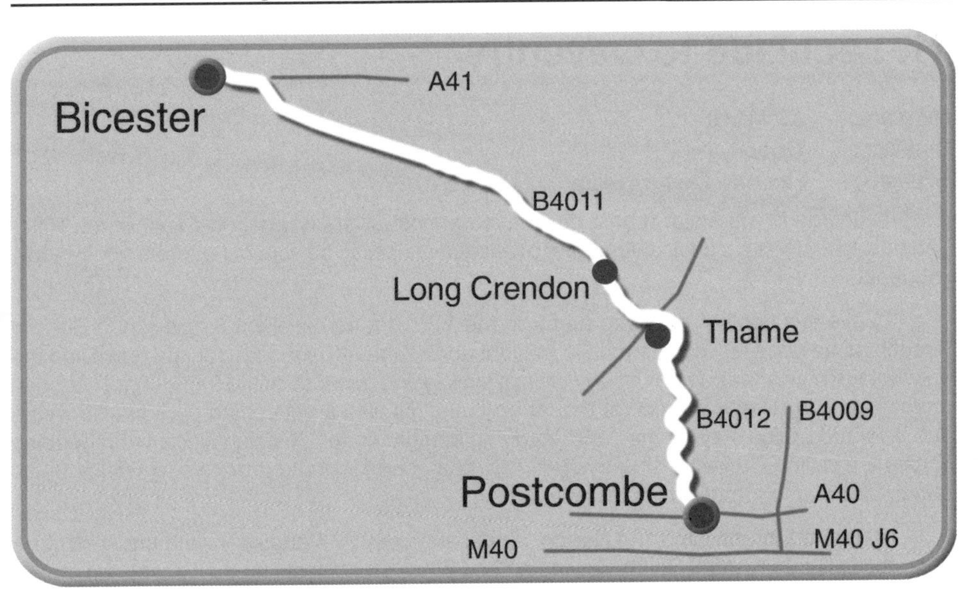

Road	Directions	Comments
A40	Oxford	Turn right just outside Postcombe onto the B4012
B4012	Thame	Turn right at Thame following 'Through Traffic' signs around the ring road
B4011	Long Crendon Bicester	At third roundabout on Thame ring road go straight on to Long Crendon
B4011	Bicester	Join the A41 shortly before Bicester
A41	Bicester	

11. Lechlade to Daventry

Distance: **51 Miles**
Surface: **Good**
Scenery: **Rolling Countryside**

Lechlade is a popular tourist destination almost at the navigational limit of the River Thames. It also has a significant number of antique shops, so beware of potterers and window shoppers.

Leave this behind and head north on the A361 for an excellent 8 mile run to Burford through some good fast sweepers. Go straight across the A40 roundabout and down into the busy village high street. This is nearly always slow-going because of the traffic light controlled bridge over the River Windrush at the far end; and it's also a pedestrian paradise so watch out. After the bridge stay on the A361, carrying straight on for Chipping Norton and heading across the rolling Cotswold countryside. This is a good fast road if there's not much traffic about, which unfortunately isn't too often.

Carry on through Chipping Norton, across the busy A44 and keep with the A361 for a good run to Banbury. After South Newington and Bloxham (look out for the Gatso), the outline of Banbury appears on the horizon and soon you'll have to turn left and follow the A4260 down into the town centre. Go straight across at the Banbury Cross roundabout and the major crossroads just after, and then you'll be heading through the commercial and industrial northern outskirts. At the next roundabout go right following the signs for the M40. When you get to the motorway, go on to the roundabout and take the second exit which should have you back on the A361 and heading towards Daventry.

Now you're off and running again, but the road's a bit narrow in places and can get very busy at times. There's some good riding along this section if you get the timing right, but if everything's getting too congested there are some very attractive villages along the way which can provide useful "break" points if the traffic density gets a bit too much. At the end of the road you meet the A45 as it swings around Daventry, which is not too surprising as there's not a great deal of interest here.

A361 Near Banbury

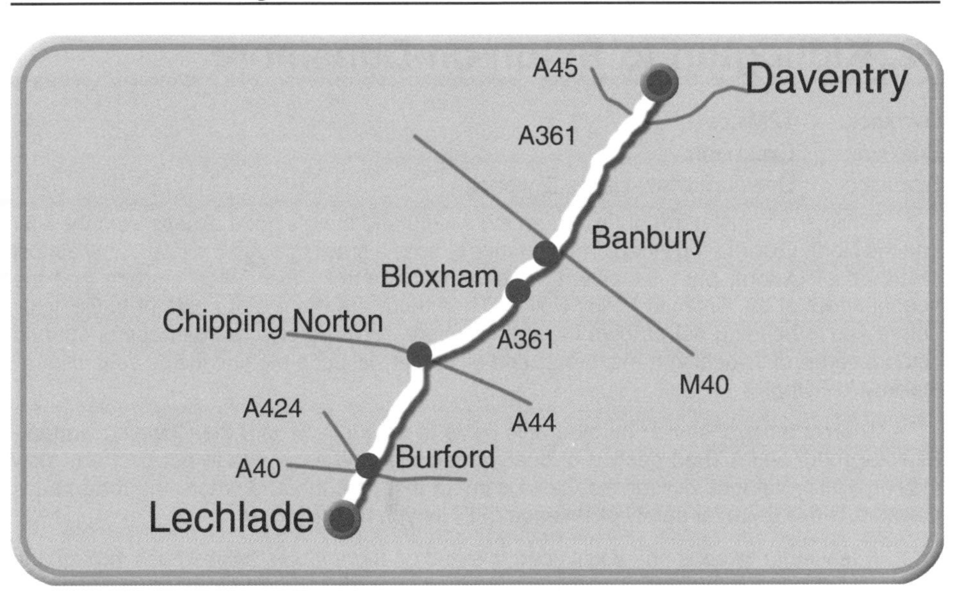

Road	Direction	Comments
A361	Burford	Across roundabout at the A40 and through the town centre. Keep to the A361
A361	Chipping Norton	Through Chipping Norton
A361	Banbury	Gatso at Bloxham. Follow the the A4260 into the town centre
A422	M40	At town centre straight over Banbury Cross roundabout then follow signs for the M40
A361	Daventry	At the M40 roundabout take the A361. Meet the A45 just before Daventry and continue into town if you wish

12. Kidlington to Ryton-on-Dunsmore

DISTANCE: 42MILES
SURFACE: EXCELLENT
SCENERY: OPEN COUNTRY, FIELDS & WOODS

Kidlington is just north of Oxford on the A4260 and there's good access from the A34 and the North Oxford Ring Road. The first mile or so is a crawl through the town, now almost a suburb of Oxford, past SavaCentre - cheap(ish) petrol - the Gatso camera and the headquarters of the Thames Valley Police. Then there are three more sets of traffic lights before you're heading out of town towards Banbury. Immediately, the road opens out and starts a series of sweeping turns, crests and dips, that will put a big grin inside your visor all the way to Ryton.

There's a petrol station by the traffic lights at the junction with the Chipping Norton - Bicester road, and a short section of dual carriageway will allow you to get past any slow moving traffic, but look out for the Gatso camera just past the end where the road heads downhill. Is this there for safety or revenue? - I'll let you be the judge!

A few more sweeps and you'll need to stand on the anchors as you pass through the village of Deddington, but then it's off again for more grins all the way to Adderbury. The traffic lights here mark the start of what's usually a crawl through Banbury. Over the years Banbury has managed to wipe out nearly all of it's interesting buildings and historical monuments. Cromwell demolished the castle in 1646, the cross of nursery rhyme fame went in 1602 - the present one is a 19th Century replica - and the old canal wharf has now been replaced by a shopping mall.

Keep straight on, following the A423 and Southam at all junctions and roundabouts, and sooner or later you'll pass the aluminium factory on the right. Banbury's now behind you and you're back into open country again. A new bridge takes you over the M40 and the road continues its sweeping course north. South of Ladbroke the road narrows slightly and there's a wonderful series of bends that run into each other before a newish section of road takes you to the east of the village, a once infamous accident black spot.

A423 AT LADBROKE

Southam looms large on the horizon, but a new bypass means that you can keep going past a useful petrol station and on into Long Itchington. Two pubs on either side of the canal make this a pleasant place to take a break, or you can continue on to Marston where there's more of the same.

At Princethorpe, the Fosse Way Roman Road crosses the A423 at the bottom of a curving dip, so keep a good look out for unsighted traffic joining and leaving. From here there's only a few more curves left before the road straightens and heads almost arrow-like for the last couple of miles to the junction with the A46. The Peugeot factory is on the right here, and there will be a lot of traffic around at shift changes.

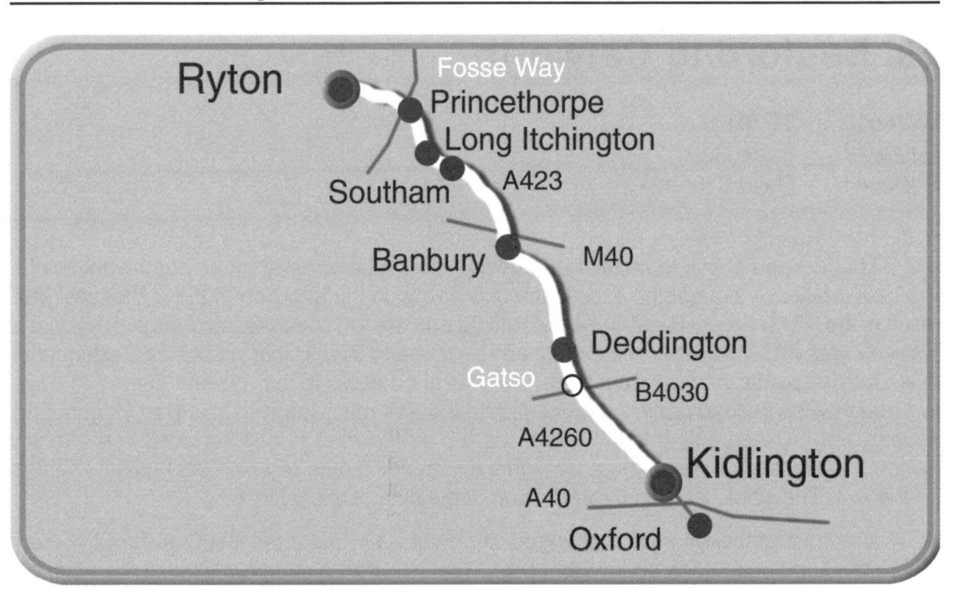

Road	Direction	Comments
A4260	Deddington Banbury	Gatso 2 miles north of the B4030 crossroads
A4260	Banbury	Straight on in Banbury
A423	Southam	Follow Southam signs out of Banbury, bypass Southam on the A423
A423	Ryton	Long Itchington is a good place for a break or keep going, careful at Princethorpe where the Fosse Way crosses the A423

13. Bedford to Catworth

DISTANCE: **18 MILES**
SURFACE: **EXCELLENT**
SCENERY: **OPEN COUNTRY**

The first part of this route up to Kimbolton used to be a real stormer, but the antics of a few have obviously bought the excellence of this road to the attention of the authorities. The result is the 'B660 Safety Road Scheme' with 30 and 40mph speed restrictions everywhere a property gets within 20 yards of the road, and an unmarked police car with camera equipment that's out on patrol at most weekends. But the good news is that no-one seems to have realised that the second part from Kimbolton to the A14 past Catworth is almost as good! So as long as you're careful, it is still worth the trip as the road is well surfaced and offers a wonderful selection of twists, turns, straights and bends, some of which interestingly tighten on the exit. The whole lot runs through open undulating countryside.

Just east of the Bedford rugby ground on the A421, take the B660 at the St. Peters roundabout and head north on the Kimbolton Road. There's a short run to clear the outskirts of Bedford and after 1½ miles there's a small roundabout where you should take the second exit. Passing the Mowsbury Golf Club on the right, the road climbs and then turns sharp left. After a short straight there's a sharp right-hander that tightens and then you're into Ravensden. Bolnhurst and Keysoe Row follow quickly, as do the bends and sweeps and the annoying intermittent speed restrictions.

As thirteen miles comes up on the odometer, so does the T-junction with the B645. Turn left here towards Kimbolton and follow the brick wall that marks the boundary of the public school. As the road enters the village it narrows and turns sharp left and then an even sharper right between high walls and buildings. Look out for large vehicles using all the road (and sometimes more!) as they struggle to get round the corner. The centre of Kimbolton is like a miniature market town, with a broad but short main street, where there's a small tearoom, the village stores and a pub, as well as a few other shops. At the end of the main street, follow the road as it turns right and then sharp left, and there's a petrol station a few hundred yards further on.

Just past this turn right, back onto the B660 for the 3 mile run in to Catworth. In contrast to the previous section, this is much straighter (and quicker) but it still has some interesting bends and curves to keep the attention levels up as the road traverses a much flatter landscape. There's another petrol station in Catworth (and a pub) and the narrow road leaves the village descending between high hedges to the junction with the A14 a mile further up the road. Turn right here onto the slip road to join the A14 towards Thrapston and the next route from Islip to Corby. Or turn round and head back to Bedford.

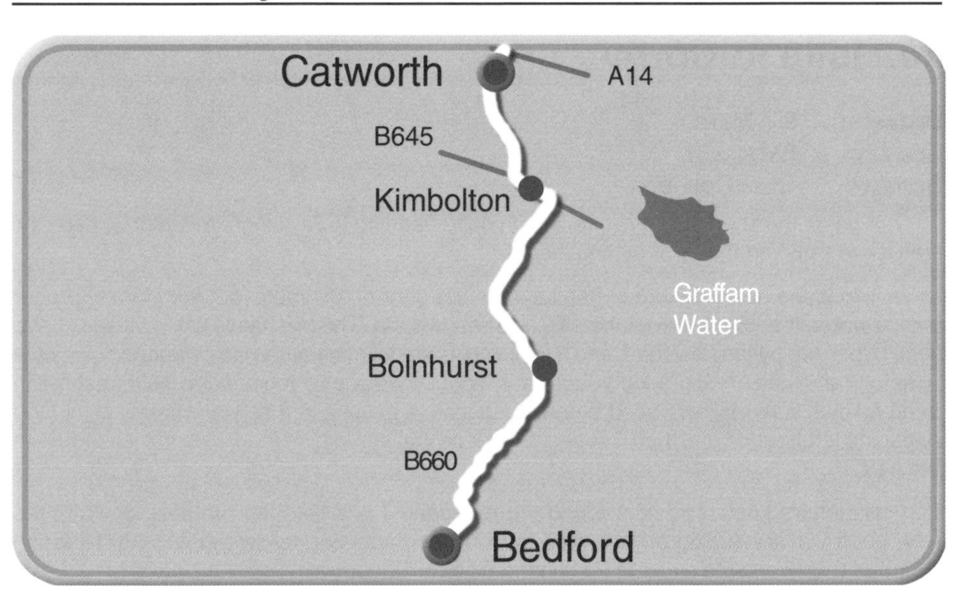

Road	Direction	Comments
B660	Kimbolton	Head North on Kimbolton Road from St Peters roundabout
B660	Kimbolton	After 1.5 miles, second exit at roundabout
B645	Kimbolton	Left at the T-junction with the B645, through Kimbolton and turn right past the petrol station for Catworth
B660	Catworth	Past Catworth turn right onto the slip road for the A14 towards Kettering and take Route 14, Islip to Corby

14. Islip to Corby

DISTANCE: 9.7 MILES
SURFACE: EXCELLENT
SCENERY: OPEN COUNTRY

A bit on the short side this one, but if you're heading to Rockingham Motor Speedway, then there's no better way of getting there.

Islip is the nearest point of habitation to the start of this route, but the journey proper begins where the A6116 leaves the A14 and heads north. The few hamlets and villages have been bypassed by the new road, and it gets into its stride immediately as it sweeps down past Lowstock and then around Sudborough, which both have pubs if you need some refreshment. Bend follows curve follows bend before Brigstock is passed in a similar manner by a long sweeping left-hander, and then a series of sweeps that carries the road up to the junction with the A43.

Hedonists should go right round the roundabout and take the run back down to the A14, but if you're heading off to a race meeting turn right and follow the A43/A6116 to the centre of Corby and the signs to Rockingham Motor Speedway.

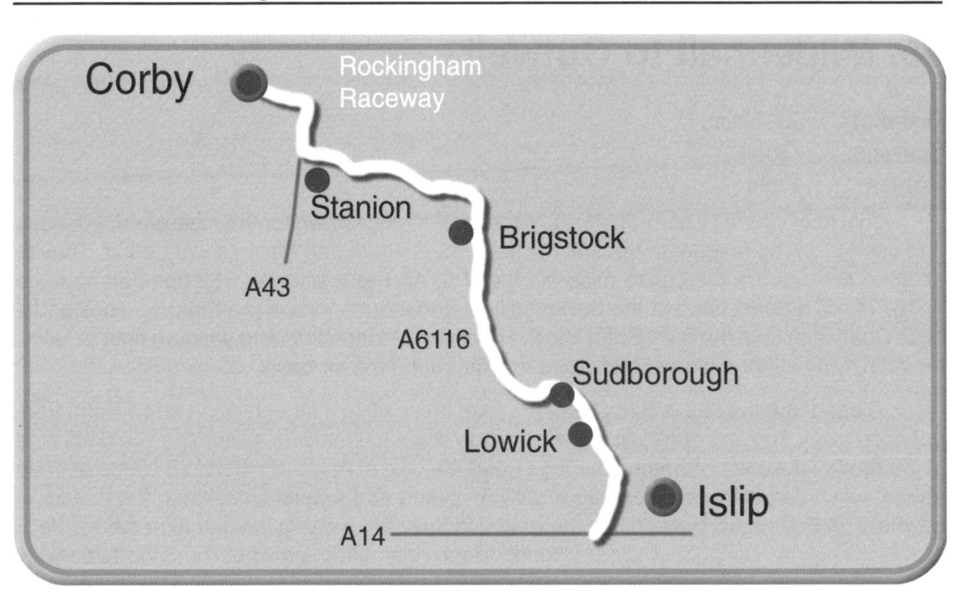

Road	Direction	Comments
A6116	Corby	Straight on past Lowick, Sudborough, Brigstock to Stanion
A43	Corby	Turn right onto the A43 for Corby and follow signs for Rockingham Raceway if that is your destination, or turn round and head straight back!

15. Mildenhall to Outwell

Distance: **27 Miles**
Surface: **Good**
Scenery: **Fens**

Just down the A11 from Thetford, Mildenhall is best known for the massive USAF base that used to act as magnet to the anti-nuclear protesters during the cold war period. They're all gone now, as are the cruise missiles, the U.S. Air Force and the B52 bombers, but the A1101 is still around. Start at the Barton Mills roundabout on the A11 - three garages and a Little Chef - and take the Bury Road into the centre of Mildenhall where you turn right to follow the A1101 to Littleport along Field Road and out round the air base.

Clear of the houses in Beck Row, the road takes off in a straight line across Burnt Fen, but keep away from the edges as it's a long drop down to the fields, assuming you don't land in the muddy dyke first. Stretch your legs - and the bike's. And then there's a clump of trees ahead which suddenly resolves into a railway station and a level crossing in the middle of nowhere. But even more surprising the road suddenly turns sharp left and then swings back round to the right, although what it's trying to avoid is anybody's guess.

A1101 at Kenny Hill

Back on the straight again and it's four miles without so much as a kink, but watch the speed as there's a nice big yellow camera where the B1382 heads off to Prickwillow and the Drainage Museum. A gentle curve right at the end of the straight brings you to the junction with the A10. Take the first exit at this roundabout, crossing the River Great Ouse and still keeping to the A1101 as it sweeps left around Littleport. At the next roundabout turn right following the A1101 as it heads in a series of short bursts straight towards to a massive high grass bank that appears to bar the way. At the last minute the road turns ninety degrees right and runs along the base of the bank, climbing to sweep left over the New and Old Bedford Rivers and past the village of Welney.

The road is now transformed and wiggles all over the place as if to make up for the straight times it's had to endure since leaving Mildenhall. At Upwell there's a T-junction where the road crosses the old course of the River Nene (now part of the navigable Welland Link), and you should turn right here for the last few miles into Outwell and the final T-junction with the A1122.

There's a petrol station a few yards to the left and plenty of places to stop and take a rest in both Outwell and Upwell. Enjoy.

Upwell

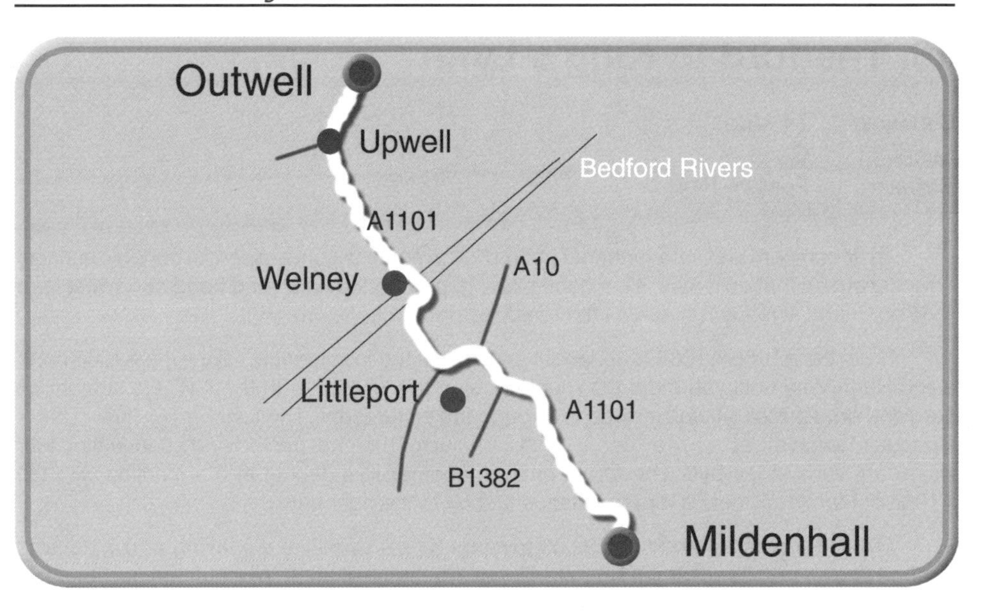

Road	Direction	Comments
A1101	Mildenhall	Take Bury Rd from Barton Mills Roundabout to Mildenhall, turn right to continue on the A1101
A1101	Littleport	Gatso where the B1382 joins. Turn left at the A10
A10	follow Cambridge	Turn right at next roundabout on the A10 heading south
A1101	Welney, Outwell Wisbech	Right at T-junction in Upwell. Cafe's, petrol etc at Upwell and Outwell

16. Thetford to King's Lynn

Distance: **24 Miles**
Surface: **Good**
Scenery: **Forest, Fens**

To all campers and caravanners Thetford is the home of some essential portable sanitary devices; but be that as it may, it's a good place to pick up the A134 and head northwest for a wide open and sweepy run across the fens.

From the A1066/A1088 roundabout just east of the town centre, follow the A1066 north along Hurth Way until you meet the roundabout at the junction with the A11. Go straight on here and onto the A134 which sweeps through the picturesque Thetford Forest Park. This is a popular tourist attraction, so keep a good look out for the unexpected and sudden stops for ice cream vans in lay-bys. The forest ends at another roundabout and a junction with the A1065 at Mumford (there's a petrol station just off to the right here).

From Mumford the road strikes off towards King's Lynn like a snaking arrow, passing through or by a number of small Norfolk villages where you'll need to get off the gas for a few moments. This is a really epic run, and although the scenery is a bit on the flat side, this does mean that you'll have few distractions from making good progress on the road. There are plenty of petrol stations along this stretch so don't be afraid to use the fuel in the tank.

It all comes to an end at the junction with the A10 and the inevitable traffic. Turn right here for the last 4 miles to King's Lynn and the big Hardwick roundabout where you'll find all the services you could need, from a tyre to a burger (what's the difference?).

Suitably refreshed and re-fitted, why not do a complete one eighty and head on back to Thetford?

Thetford Forest

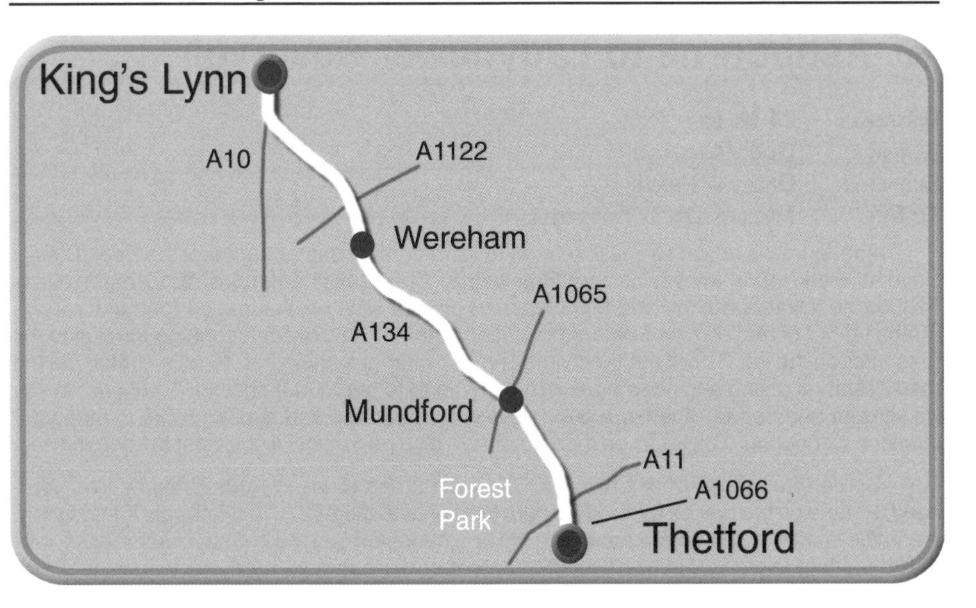

Road	Direction	Comments
A1066	North	Over roundabout at the A11 junction
A134	Mundford King's Lynn	Continue to Mundford
A134	Wereham King's Lynn	Continue on the A134 at Mundford towards Wereham
A10	King's Lynn	A134 meets the A10 and the traffic. Continue on for King's Lynn or return to Thetford!

17. Ashbourne to Ladybower Reservoir

Distance: 34 Miles
Surface: Good/Average
Scenery: Dales & Peaks
To See: Millers Dale, Tideswell

Ashbourne is an old Derbyshire market town on the southern edge of the Peak District National Park, often known as the 'Gateway to the Peaks'. Take the A515 north out of Ashbourne towards Buxton and Manchester. This is a wide, well-surfaced road that quickly climbs up out of the town and enters the national park, with Dovedale running parallel to the road over on the left. There are plenty of elevation changes along this 17 mile stretch, as the road assumes a single-minded approach in its need to get to Manchester. That's not to say it's straight and boring - there's a good selection of sweeps and sudden kinks to stop your attention wandering. The traffic on this section will also need work if you want to keep moving.

Some three miles from Buxton as the road drops down towards Brierlow Bar, you'll need to stand on the brakes for the tight right hander onto the A5270 to Blackwell. Immediately, the traffic is behind you as the road narrows and heads off into the countryside for a 2½ mile 'warm up' that takes you to the T-junction with the A6. Turn right here and follow the A6 for half-a-mile before turning left onto the B6049 that takes you past Blackwell and on down towards Miller's Dale in the deep valley of the River Wye, with its high brick-arched railway viaduct. This is wonderfully twisty and the scenery is superb.

Tideswell is just up the twisting road and all services can be found here. The town calls itself the 'Cathedral of the Peaks' and the church is very grand if a little out of scale with its surroundings, but a cathedral...? Past Tideswell, it's a short run up to the A623 where you need to do a sharp right/left to stay on the still twisting B6049 for Bradwell. There's a petrol station in the village, but hang on for a few miles as there's a much cheaper one just up the road.

At the T-junction with the A6187, turn right and follow Hope Road along the Derwent Valley for 1½ miles to the traffic lights. The cheaper petrol station is on the left. Turn left onto the A6013 for the last part of the route, through Bamford and up to the reservoir by the junction with the A57. This is a popular place during summer weekends, so keep a good look out for the unexpected. When you get to the traffic lights by the reservoir you've got a choice of turning left for the Snake Pass and Glossop, or right for Sheffield and beyond. Of course, you could also ride the whole road back to Ashbourne.

South of Tideswell on the B6049

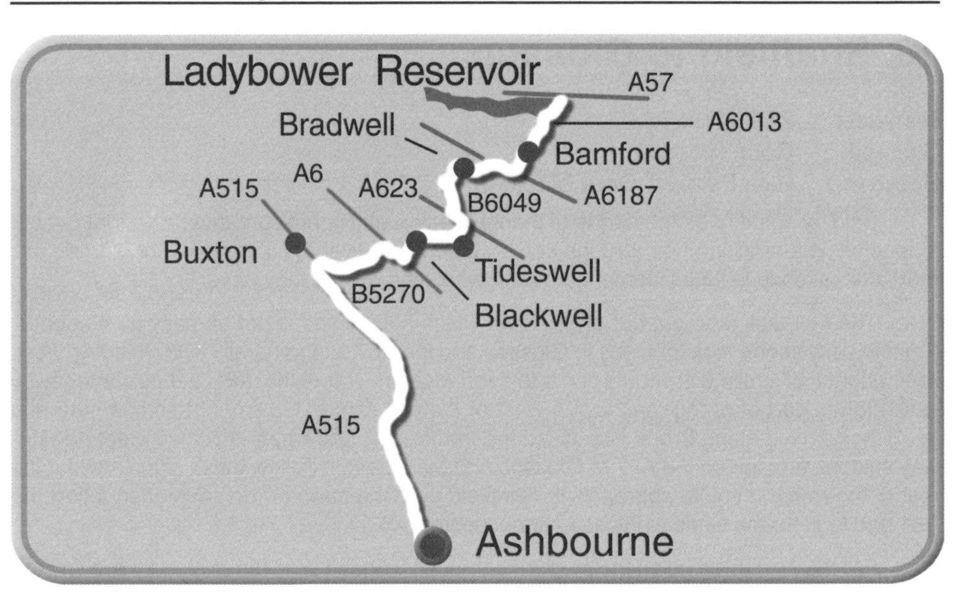

Road	Direction	Comments
A515	Buxton	Straight on until right turn onto the A5270
A5270	Blackwell	At junction with theA6 turn right for half a mile then left onto the B6049
B6049	Tideswell	Right onto the A623 then left back onto the B6049
B6049	Bradwell	At junction with the A6187 turn right for $1^1/_2$ miles to traffic lights, turn left onto the B6013
A6013	Bamford	Straight on to Ladybower reservoir

18. Sheffield to Glossop

Distance: **23.7 Miles**
Surface: **Good (mostly)**
Scenery: **High Peaks & Open Moors**

Said by some to be the daddy of them all, although I'm not sure that I'd go that far; but it certainly is a cracking ride through some stupendous scenery. Everyone should ride this road at least once in their lifetime, no matter what kind of bike they have.

The first task is to get out of Sheffield which sometimes is not as easy as it sounds. From the city centre look for signs to Glossop and the A57 and generally keep heading west. After about half a mile you should come to a roundabout. This is the A61, a dual carriageway which forms part of a ring-road to the west of the city centre. Go straight across here and you'll be heading along Brook Hill. Avoid the tramtracks, and where the road enters a one-way system, turn left on the A57 to Glossop and Manchester. Follow these signs now for the rest of the route. If you're approaching Sheffield from the north or the south then follow the A61 and look for the signs to Glossop, Manchester (A57).

For the next three miles the road runs through wooded suburbs (watch for the Gatso), but by the time the A6101 joins from the right at Rivelin, the houses have been left behind and you're at the edge of the Peak District National Park. The road's not particularly wide here, the surface isn't stunningly smooth and there can be quite a bit of traffic around especially on summer weekends, but the bends come straight at you as the road climbs into ever more rugged surroundings before dropping unexpectedly down to the Ladybower Reservoir. Even more surprising is the set of traffic lights where the A6103 from Bamford comes in from the left.

Go straight on here, following a wider and better surfaced road along the northern edge of the reservoir, but keep a look out for cars popping in and out of the parking spaces by the water's edge. After 2½ miles the reservoir's left behind and the road narrows and resumes it's climb to the summit of Snake Pass. There's some pretty tricky corners along here and on some the surface has taken a real hard pounding, and where the road runs through the woods the surface can stay damp for a long time after any rainfall. Before the summit, the Snake Pass Inn provides a welcome break, but the best is yet to come as the road tops the high moorland and runs around Featherbed Top before descending rapidly towards the Cheshire Plain. This is a technically challenging road with some staggering scenery, and it takes no prisoners.

Snake Pass Summit

The town of Glossop brings forward motion to a grinding halt, so stop off at the Tasty Bite Cafe for refreshments before doing the whole lot again on the run back to Sheffield.

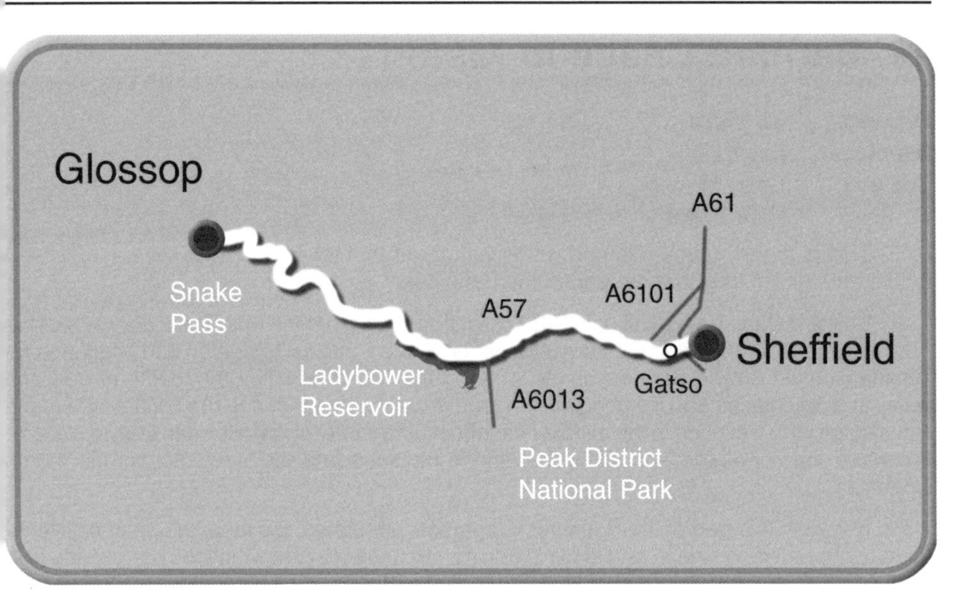

Road	Direction	Comments
A57	Glossop	From the City Centre follow signs for Glossop, straight over the A61 roundabout, turn left on the A57 to Glossop.
A57	Glossop	Note Gatso in suburbs of Sheffield
A57	Glossop	Straight on at the traffic lights at Ladybower reservoir where the A6103 joins from the left
A57	Glossop	Snake Pass, and on in to Glossop

19. Barnard Castle to Alston

Distance: **32 Miles**
Surface: **Excellent**
Scenery: **Open Moors**
To See: **High Force**

This is a particularly wild and windswept route that takes you over the west Durham moors and fells of this northern part of the Pennines.

Barnard Castle is a bustling market town that sits above the river Tees just north of the A66. Stay south of the river and carry straight on at the lights for Mickleton and Middleton-in-Teesdale on the B6277. Running up the length of the Teesdale valley, the road is narrow and twisty in many places and it's popular with tourists and walkers during the holiday season. It can also be very wet even in the middle of summer, and winter snowfalls often lead to closure. But when the conditions are right the riding is fabulous and the views across the moors incredible.

Although this part of the Pennines is sparsely populated, the land has been cultivated for many hundreds of years, and at Mickleton it's still possible to see the long narrow ridges in the fields that resulted from medieval strip-farming methods. Past here, the road crosses the river and snakes up through the old mining town of Middleton-in-Teesdale, with the old stone quarries to the west at Holwick Scars still visible from the road.

Leaving Middleton behind, the road continues up Teesdale with the views becoming more dramatic by the mile. Opposite the High Force Hotel a footpath leads off to High Force, a spectacular waterfall that plunges 70ft over the Great Whin Sill escarpment. There's a car park alongside the hotel (£1 - but they will look after your helmet and jacket), and entrance to the falls costs £1 (tickets from the gift shop). Once you get to the foot of the falls, the strenuous can take a further path that takes you right up to an overlook above the falls. Back on two-wheels, the road finally leaves all traces of civilisation behind and continues its climb onto the lonely moors. This is not a place for a break down - but if you do, you'll have plenty of time to take in the outstanding scenery. This is some exceptional riding, but do keep a wary eye on the road surface as it is not all billiard table smooth. And use the snow poles to track the road's direction.

High Force

With Burnhope Seat on one side and Round Hill on the other, the road straightens out as it makes for the small village of Garrigill. The road swings round to the east to avoid disturbing the solitude of the old stone houses, the one shop, the church and the imposing Congregational Chapel set around the spacious green, before straightening out and running down into Alston. This old market town claims to be the highest in England, and I certainly wouldn't dispute that, especially considering the steep slope of the cobbled main street. Be very, very careful if it's wet.

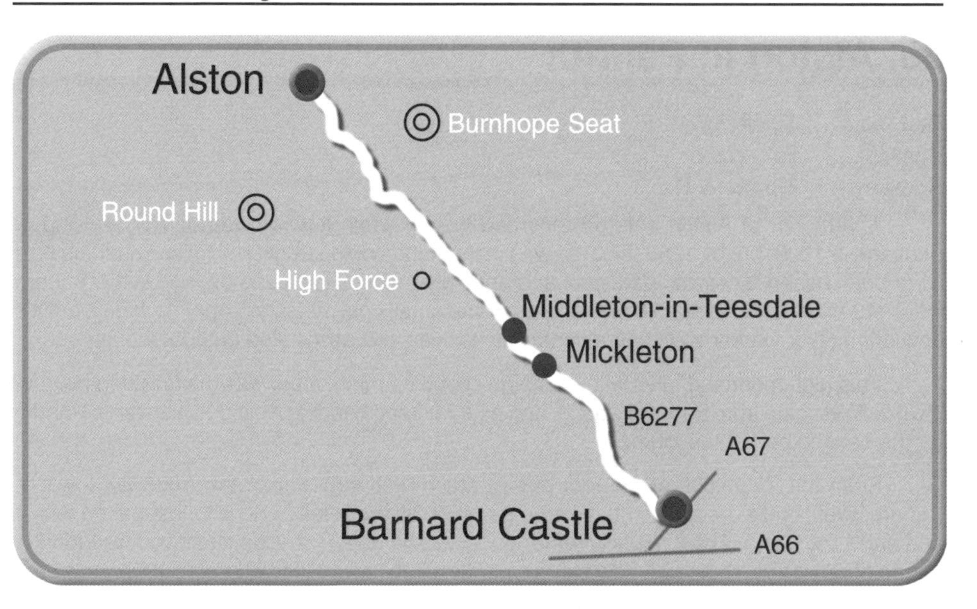

Road	Direction	Comments
B6277	Mickleton Alston	Up the Teesdale valley from Barnard Castle through Mickleton and Middleton
B6277		High Force waterfall about 4 miles from Middleton
B6277	Alston	Follow the road to Alston - Burnhope Seat on the right, Round Hill on your left.

Burnhope Seat

20. Alston to Penrith

Distance: 19 Miles
Surface: Excellent
Scenery: Moors & Hills

The manor of Alston entered recorded history when it was given to William King of Scotland in 1209; but by 1280 the area was in the hands of the English. The surrounding fells have been mined for silver, lead, coal and anthracite since Roman times, and in 1718 there were 119 mines producing £70,000 a year. Some small coal mines still operate today, but it's now primarily a market town and a centre for walking and associated outdoor industries.

This high moorland town with its steeply cobbled main street was the finishing point of the previous route from Barnard Castle, and now we keep heading west down towards Penrith for the second part of the journey.

From the T-junction at the foot of that steep high street, take the A686 left towards Penrith. Well, that's the directions taken care of, so all that's left to do is to just get on with it and enjoy the riding. And it really is rather good. A mile down the road takes you through the village of Bayles and the route now starts a gentle climb towards the edge of the Pennine Hills and takes some wonderful sweeping turns to get there.

And then at a height of 1,900 feet, the road suddenly sweeps round hard to the right at Hartside, passing a big cafe on your left that's a popular watering hole and you're at the edge of the hills and starting the descent. Look out as there's a tight hairpin left coming up, then the road twists and turns across open ground before reaching the edge of the Eden Valley. Now it hugs the edges of the high ground as it makes its way down to the valley below. From the earlier sweeps it's now all twists and turns as the road runs around rock outcrops in a way that's not much different from a ride through the Alps or the Pyrenees. There's a good five miles of this before the road opens out as it reaches Melmerby, but this only means that the pace can be quickened, on through Langwathby and down to the A6 roundabout at Penrith.

Melmerby dates back to the 9th century, when it was believed to have taken its name from Melmor, a Dane who lived in the area. But Penrith goes way back to 500 BC when it was a Celtic settlement. By the 10th century it was the capital of the Scottish kingdom of Strathclyde.

A686 below Hartside

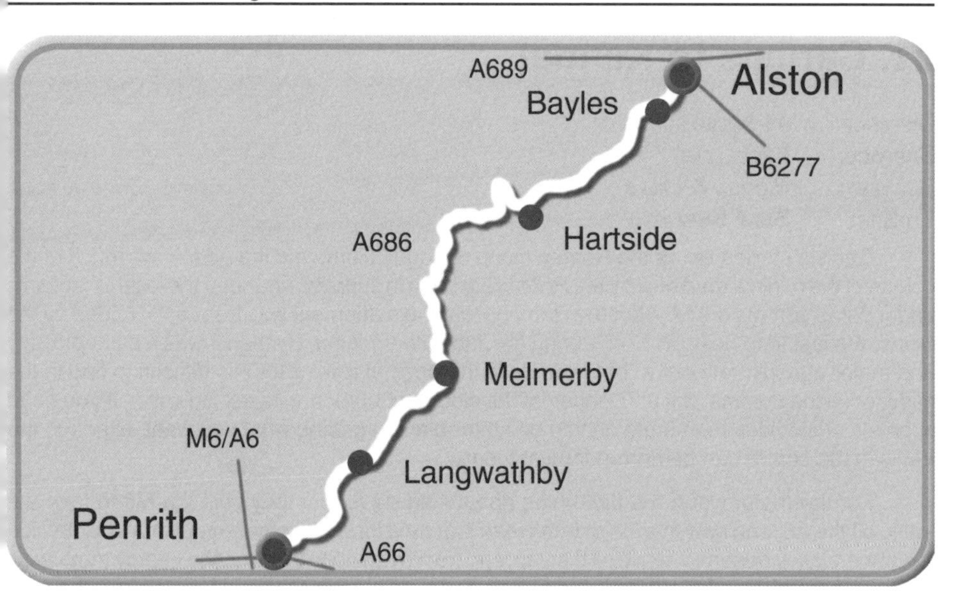

Road	Direction	Comments
A686	Penrith	From the T-junction at the foot of the steep, cobbled High Street take the A686 and follow it all the way to Penrith
A686		Café at Hartside
A686		Join the A6 or A66 at Penrith

21. Carlisle to Kendal

DISTANCE: 41 MILES
SURFACE: EXCELLENT
SCENERY: MOORS & HILLS
TO SEE: SHAP SUMMIT

Carlisle started life as the Roman camp of Luguvalium, and the A6 follows much of the course of the original road built by the Romans to bring in supplies and keep the local inhabitants under some sort of control. After the Romans left, the settlement was frequently raided by the Scots, the last time being in 1745 during the Jacobite uprising. By then it was a cathedral city and major agricultural centre, but nowadays the original town centre is difficult to find in the midst of all the commercial and industrial development of recent years. However, if you need supplies or services then there should be no problem in getting what you want, although the traffic in the centre can be horrendous at times.

For the motorcyclist the best thing about Carlisle is that they built the M6 to take the traffic off the A6, and now this major trunk road that runs through some exceptional countryside is comparatively deserted, while all the cars and trucks are nose to tail on the nearby motorway. Enjoy it while you can, before too many people find out what they've been missing and abandon the motorway crawl to spoil all our fun.

ON THE A6 NORTH OF KENDAL

Pick up the road at junction 42 of the M6 motorway and head south young man. The ex-trunk road is wide, well-surfaced and pretty straight, and most of the bends are long sweepers on the first part of the run down to Penrith. This old market town with its red sandstone buildings is easily negotiated as the road stays well away to the east of the centre, but there's a good selection of pubs and cafes close to hand if you want to take a break.

South of Penrith things start getting a lot more interesting. That's the Lake District over there on the right, and as the hills start to move in on you, the valley has to be shared with the motorway and the railway line as all three wend their way up to the summit at Shap, a dour village that has little recommend itself to the traveller, but it's notorious for the steep climb of the adjacent railway line and the difficulties that the early steam trains had in making the ascent - and sometimes the descent as well! South of Shap the road starts its own descent towards Kendal, leaving the M6 and the railway to keep each other company off to the east. Left to its own devices, the A6 gets all twisty as it negotiates the many streams and becks that run off the hills around here, so get down with it and enjoy because all too soon it seems, the 'Welcome to Kendal' sign appears at the side of the road.

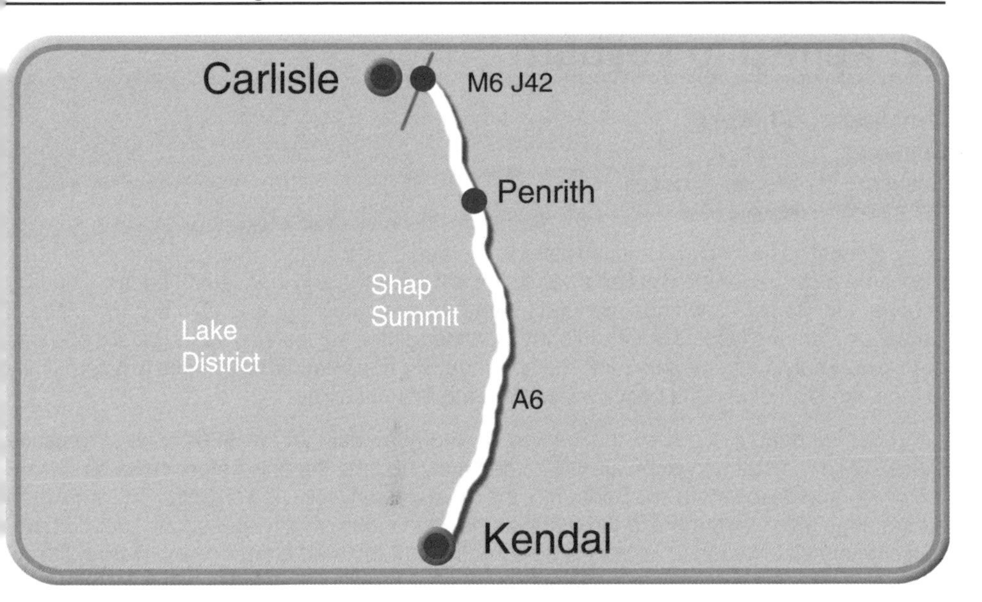

Road	Direction	Comments
A6	Penrith	Start from Junction 42 of the M6 and take the A6 through Penrith to Kendal!
A6	Kendal	Shap Summit marks the highest point

22. Kendal to Leyburn

Distance: **43 Miles**
Surface: **Good**
Scenery: **Moors & Dales**
To See: **Hawes**

Kendal has a long and ancient history; Richard Coeur de Lion made it a barony in 1189, it became a centre for the woollen trade in the 14th century, and then later it became equally important for its boot and shoe manufacturing and engineering. It was also the birthplace of Catherine Parr, the last of Henry VIII's wives, although the 12th century castle where she was born is now only a fragmentary ruin. Today Kendal is a major tourist centre due to its proximity to the Lake District and the easy access from the M6 motorway.

But we need to leave all this behind us and head east on the A684 for the Yorkshire Dales. The road starts to climb almost immediately up onto the fells before crossing the M6 motorway and descending into Sedburgh, the most westerly town in Yorkshire. The wind farm on the ridge gives testament to the fact that the wind blows steady and strong around here. The scenery all the way to Leyburn is outstanding, but the road is narrow and lined with dry-stone walls that leave no room for disagreements or errors of any sort.

A684 near Garsdale Head

Through the twists and turns of Garsdale, the road runs up the River Clough valley between Baugh Fell and Mossdale Moor, past the striking brick railway viaduct and the tempting Moorcock Inn to the village of Hawes in upper Wensleydale (great cheese, Gromit). The Pennine Way crosses here so there's going to be lot of walkers about, and when you add to that the higgledy-piggledy buildings of the village set against a most amazing scenic backdrop, you can bet the tourists will also be out in force - so take care. Unfortunately this commercialism has gone to the heads of some of the inhabitants, and if you want value-for-money then you'd be strongly advised to look elsewhere! The road runs down the whole length of Wensleydale, following the course of the River Ure and the scenery is superb. But don't get too carried away with the views as those stone walls are still awfully close and getting past the caravans, trucks and buses can be a very tight squeeze at times.

Following the River Ure, you'll come to Bainbridge, a little village of grey stone houses that face each other across a wide sloping green with the road cutting through the centre in a series of 90-degree bends. Further on, Aysgarth is another typical Dales village, but by now the drama of the surroundings is beginning to peter out as the landscape becomes flatter and more rounded the further east you travel. The sleepy village of Wensley that gave its name to this awesome valley is surprisingly uninspiring, and it's difficult to believe that it was once the principal market town for the area. By the time you get to Leyburn there's little left to remind you of the views and the road that you've just been down - except that is for those dry-stone walls!

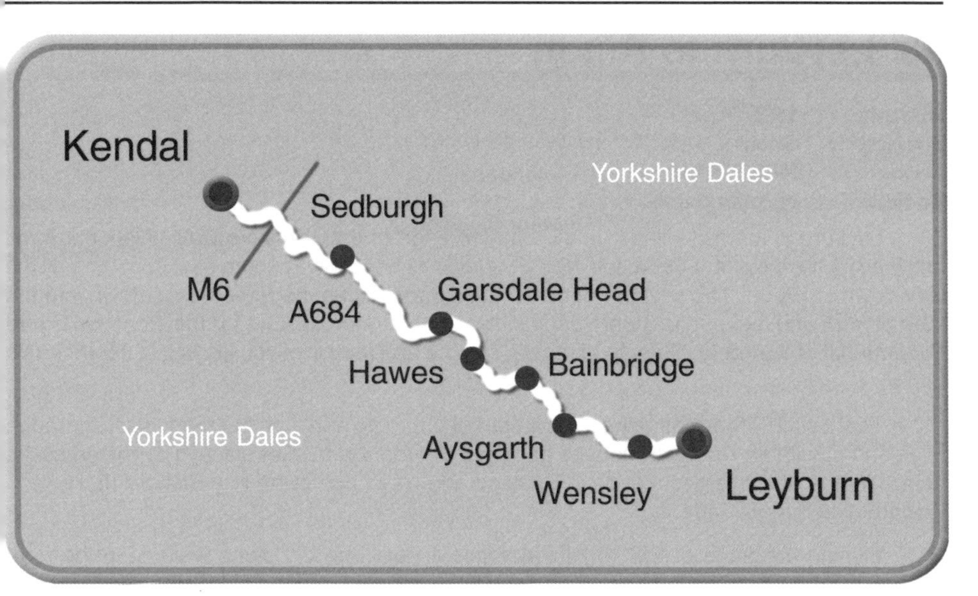

Road	Direction	Comments
A684	Sedbergh	Climb up onto the fells, cross the M6 and descend into Sedburgh
A684	Leyburn	Continue along the A684 through spectacular scenery with lots of twists and turns all the way to Leyburn

A QUIET DAY IN HAWES

23. Leyburn to Ripon

Distance: **19.5 Miles**
Surface: **Good**
Scenery: **Moors & Dales**
To See: **Masham Brewery**

Leyburn is a small village on the eastern edge of the Yorkshire Dales National Park, and leaving the excellent A684, the A6108 wiggles its narrow way south east from here all the way down to Ripon. The scenery becomes less dramatic as the route heads down into the Vale of York and leaves the moors behind, but keep a good lookout for the stone walls that border most of the route. Stray too far from the line and they'll let you know it in no uncertain terms!

There's a BP fuel station just at the start of the route and then the road passes through Middleham, with its Georgian houses gathered around the market place. The ruined castle here has one of the largest keeps in England and was once owned by Richard III. His son Edward died here in 1484.

Skirting the edge of the Yorkshire National Park, the dry stone walls take the road through the drowsy village of East Witton and its rectangular green before straightening out a tad and running past the ruins of Jervaulx Abbey. Founded by the Cistercians back in the 12th century, like many others it came under the (sledge)hammer of Henry VIII when he took England away from the Catholic church, although enough of the ruins remain to allow the layout of the church and other buildings to be traced.

The Black Sheep Brewery, Masham

From here to Masham, the road wiggles through the countryside with the moors and dales receding behind and the countryside becoming more rolling and pastoral. The walls are still in evidence though, and some of them tend to drop their stones in the road. Masham offers a welcome respite from all that hauling the bike from side to side, not least because of its brewery! If you've got the time it's well worth taking a tour of the Black Sheep Brewery, although you may need to book ahead as it gets very busy in the summer. Phone 01765-680100 to make a reservation or contact them through their website at www.blacksheepbrewery.com.

We're halfway to Ripon now, and from here the road continues through West Tanfield and North Stanley in a non-direct manner that will stop your shoulders seizing up from under-use. By the time you get to the T-junction with North Road on the outskirts of Ripon you'll probably be in need of a break, so turn right for Ripon and a well-earned rest.

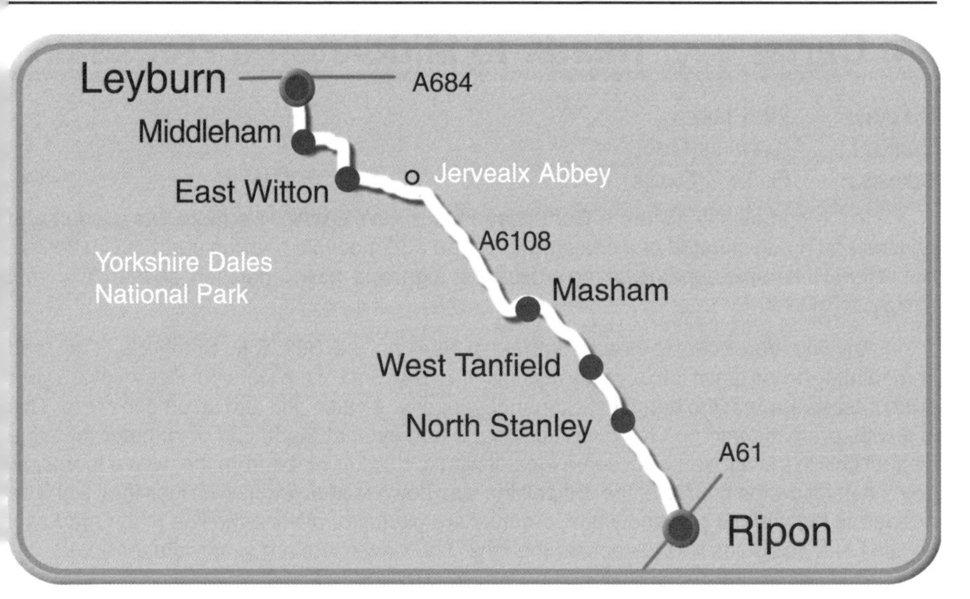

Road	Direction	Comments
A6108	Ripon	Turn off the A684 at Leyburn onto the A6108. Petrol station at Leyburn
A6108		Black Sheep Brewery at Masham
A6108	Ripon	Take a break from all those bends at Ripon - turn right at the T-junction for the town centre

24. Carterway Heads to Middleton-in-Teesdale

Distance: **22.5 Miles**
Surface: **Average/Good**
Scenery: **Fells & Dales**

To be completely accurate Carterway Heads isn't a town, it's more like a couple of houses and a pub situated at a crossroads on the A68 a couple of miles north of Castleside. But at least the name appears on the crossroads sign, and in big letters too, so there's no real excuse to miss it.

Anyway, you need to head south west here on the B6278 to Stanhope. The road immediately drops down into a valley and with the head wall of the Derwent Reservoir on your right, passes through the hamlet of Edmundbyers over a cattle grid and up onto the fells. This is a wild, dramatic and god-forsaken landscape and even at the height of summer there's a distinct chill in the air. You'll get some idea of what it's like in winter from the twelve foot snow poles that follow the course of the road all the way down to Middleton. With luck they won't be needed to dig you out of a snow drift, but they are useful for plotting the line of the road as it wiggles and squiggles it's way across the fells. The views here are simply stupendous.

High on the Fells

Crawleyside village and another cattle grid marks the far side of the fell, and the road descends abruptly back to civilisation in Stanhope and a junction with the A689. Turn right here for two hundred yards and then turn left back onto the B6278 towards Middleton and Barnard Castle. The road turns sharp right, running parallel to the main road along the bank of the infant River Wear, before doing a 180 degree left, crossing a narrow bridge to the opposite bank and going all the way back down the other side. Then it turns right, climbs steeply, crosses a cattle grid and heads back onto the fells and the snow poles for more wild and barren scenery.

Descending the far side of the fell, with Teesdale valley ahead, you'll see a small "triangular" junction on the right, signposted to Middleton. Take it. The road crosses a small stone culvert and another cattle grid, and you're into the Dales with dry-stone walls along road and sweeping views across the rolling countryside. At the T-junction turn left and follow the road down to the centre of Middleton and the junction with the B6277. There's a couple of cafes and pubs in this pretty Dales town along with all the usual services - even a bank! Parking's not too difficult, although the town does get very busy on summer weekends. There's a filling station $^{1}/_{2}$ mile further up the B6277 towards Alston.

Middleton High Street

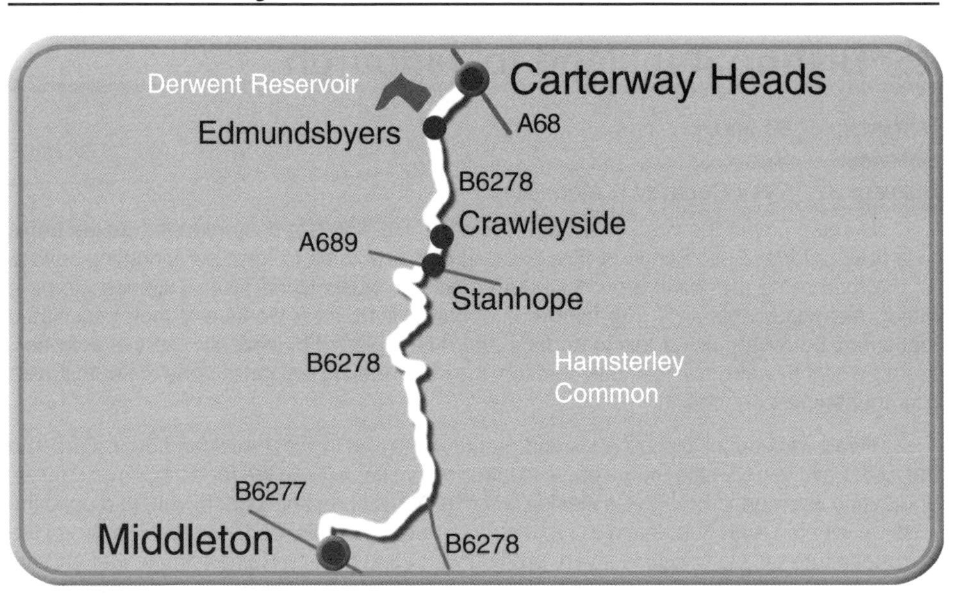

Road	Direction	Comments
B6278	Stanhope	Start from the A68 by Derwent Reservoir and turn south onto the B6278
B6278	Edmundsbury	Cattlegrid marks start of fells, ends at Crawleyside cattle grid
A689	Alston	Turn right on the A689 for 200 yards, then left back onto the B6278
B6278	Middleton Barnard Castle	Sharp bends leaving Stanhope
No number	Middleton	Right turn at the triangle on the far side of the fells
No number	Middleton	Left at the T-junction into Middleton

25. Bishop Auckland to Jedburgh

DISTANCE: **80 MILES**
SURFACE: **GOOD**
SCENERY: **OPEN COUNTRY & MOORLAND**

Starting just to the west of Bishop Auckland, the A68 is a busy road that takes traffic over the border and into Scotland. The first part of the route up to Tow Law is nothing special as the road skirts the areas around Durham and Newcastle-Upon-Tyne. This used to be a major heavy industrial area with hundreds of coal mines, steel works and their associated industries; but with most of this long gone and now replaced by new commercial activities, there's a slightly run-down feel to everything, the same feeling you get in parts of South Wales now that the pits are closed.

Head west out of Bishop Auckland on the A688 and in West Auckland bear right onto the A68. Past Tow Low the moors begin to intrude from the left and the road begins its snakey, undulating way north, through Castleside with the Derwent reservoir on the left, and up to the junction with the A69. Turn left at the roundabout and follow this road for about 3 miles to the Corbridge turn off. Corbridge is a very pretty town dating back to Roman times, that attracts hundreds of tourists on a summer's weekend. It also has the last petrol station before the Scottish border over 30 miles away, and that one up on the moors charges exorbitant prices!

Head north from Corbridge on the A68, and about 2½ miles further on, just past the next roundabout you cross the line of Hadrian's Wall. This was built in around 122 AD. under the orders of the Roman Emperor of the same name to defend the northern frontier of his British province from the Picts and the Scots. It doesn't seem to work any more!

DESCENDING THE DERWENT VALLEY NORTH OF CASTLESIDE

With all this Roman activity in the area, it's not too surprising to know that the A68 follows the course of an earlier Roman road. And with their predilection for travelling in straight lines, there's some serious crests and dips along here as the road pursues its single-minded approach to taking the shortest distance from A to B, with scant regard to the undulating landscape. There's also some seriously wild and desolate scenery along here as we head across the moors towards the Northumberland National Park and the junction with the A696. Turn left here and continue on the A68, following the valley of the River Rede and climbing over the Cheviot Hills and past Catcleugh Reservoir to the English-Scottish border at Carter Bar. From here the road descends through some tight curves down to the border town of Jedburgh.

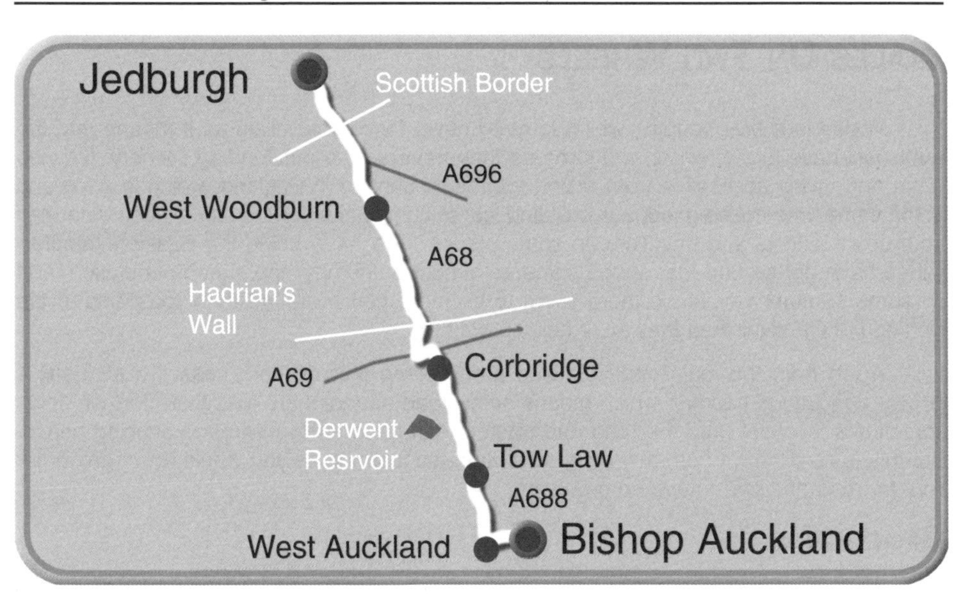

Road	Direction	Comments
A688	Barnard Castle	Head West and turn off at West Auckland onto the A68
A68	Tow Law Corbridge	Derwent reservoir on left
A69	Corbridge	Turn left onto the A69 and right back onto the A68 after 3 miles. Last petrol before Jedburgh
A68	Jedburgh	2.5 miles North of the A69 is Hadrian's Wall
A68	Jedburgh	Turn left at junction with the A696 and continue on to Jedburgh

Wales On Two Wheels

Wales is a hilly country, which is good news for motorcyclists as it means that the roads will have lots of twists and turns as they traverse the outstanding scenery. It's also close and easily accessible from major population centres in England, which is good and at the same time not so good, as you'll find lots of competition for the same piece of tarmac from other tourists and travellers. In some places - the A470 being the classic example - things have got so bad that speed cameras almost outnumber the sheep population, and on some summer weekends there seem to be more police around than you'd find at the Notting Hill Carnival. And they have helicopters too!

Apart from the major industrialised areas along the southern coast it's also still a largely agricultural country, which means some road surfaces are less than perfect, fields sometimes 'escape' onto the road and tractors can lie in ambush around enticing bends. But this is no different from any other rural area, so just ride as you would down any other country road and you'll have no problems.

Geography

The principality of Wales is only some 136 miles from north to south and between 37 and 92 miles in breadth, but into this small space is packed an abundance of the most spectacular scenery. The whole area is dominated by mountains composed almost entirely of rocks from the Paleozoic period, and the deep valleys that dissect them. Some of these valleys show glacial origins but a number of them are structural, brought into existence from violent earth movements many millions of years ago.

The Elan Valley

The mountainous landscape reaches its crescendo in the Snowdon massif in the northwest, and this whole area has many peaks over 2,800 ft. separated by deep valleys which are often filled by lakes. To the south and east of Snowdonia the country is still highland at around 2000 ft., but is less mountainous and is dominated by open moors. Further south, the hills are more rounded and the whole region is almost covered with boulder clay, which gives a cold wet subsoil with many bogs. Agriculture is severely limited by this poor soil and the whole area is sparsely populated as a result.

Continuing south, the plateau of pre-Carboniferous rock gives way first to Old Red Sandstone and then coal measures, to form a more varied region with outstanding hills of sandstone like Radnor forest, the Black Mountains and the Brecon Beacons. From here to the south coastal plain, the coal measures have been cut by fast flowing streams of water running off the central plateau, to create the narrow, steep sided valleys that characterise this whole area, and for a long time severely restricted communications in this part of the country. To the southwest, hard resistant bands of old rock fan out to form the spectacular headlands of the Pembrokeshire coastline, whose bays were formed by the erosion of softer rocks.

The mountainous nature of the whole country, the westerly climate and the consequent prevalence of leached soils has resulted in a somewhat impoverished vegetation, although moisture-loving species such as ferns and grasses are found in abundance. Nearly two-thirds of the countryside is grassland and a large part of the remainder is woodland, with much of this being dominated by planted coniferous trees.

Getting There

Not too difficult, this one. Just head north to Birmingham and turn left! There's no border controls or passport requirements (yet), Offa's Dyke is no longer the barrier it was designed to be, and there's even direct access from the motorway network these days with no toll charges for motorbikes on the M4 Severn Crossing. But it's far better to leave the arterial highways and head off onto the minor roads and you'll have much more fun and a far more interesting journey.

What to See

For the two-wheeled traveller, the big attraction of Wales is the combination of roads and scenery. Everyone eventually heads to Snowdonia for the most spectacular stuff, and it can get very busy around there during the holiday season, with the Llanberis Pass sometimes being at a standstill all the way from Llanrug to the junction with the A498. Get there early to avoid the crowds heading for the mountain railway. A little to the south, the country around Llyn Celyn, Lake Vyrnwy and Bala Lake shouldn't be missed, and the Elan Valley is spectacular. If the weather's a bit dodgy, then Wales has a surfeit of castles worth exploring, and don't forget the car and motorcycle museum in Porthmadog. The areas of the Brecon Beacons and Radnor forest are a scenic paradise, and if coastal scenery is your thing then the Pembrokeshire coastline is a must. The moonscape of the disused slate quarries at Blaenau Ffestiniog is a graphic example of the effect that man can have on his surroundings, more so than the effects of coal mining in the south of the country. A visit to the Big Pit at Blaenavon will show you what it was like working in the Welsh coalfields.

Chepstow Castle

Accommodation and Information

The decline in heavy industry in Wales since the second half of the 20th century and the increase in people's leisure time, led to an expansion in the tourist business that has now in turn seen its own recession as more and more people choose cheaper overseas package holidays. While Wales is no longer a traditional holiday destination for a large part of the English population, its easy access means that it's still very popular for weekend breaks. This has led to the situation where the weekday traveller can have little problem finding overnight accommodation even in the peak season, but if you decide to head west for an impromptu 'Welsh Weekend' in the season you're very likely to find just about everything booked up solid. This is especially true on public holidays. The answer to this, as always, is to book ahead.

There's plenty of accommodation to be found in Wales. In the larger towns and resorts along the coast you'll find hotels, guesthouses and private bed & breakfast establishments. Hotels and B&Bs can be booked by the day, but guesthouses are more geared towards periods of one week or more. Away from the major centres your choice will be limited to bed & breakfast or half-board accommodation in either private houses or inns. The latter are usually excellent value, and you're saved all the hassle of finding somewhere for a drink in the evening after a good days riding. There's also a good selection of self-catering accommodation, ranging from caravans and chalets on organised sites, to farmhouses, but these are usually only bookable on a weekly basis. If there's a group of you and you don't mind sharing the household duties, then self-catering offers a lot of flexibility and is very cost-effective. Whatever type of accommodation you decide to choose, then the best place to start is with the local tourist authority.

Tourist Board/Information	Website Address
Welsh Touurist Board	www.visitwales.com
Mid & West Coast Wales	www.mid-wales-tourism.org.uk
North Wales Tourism	www.nwt.co.uk
South Wales Tourism	www.south-wales.org.uk
Smoothhound UK Accommodation booking service	www.smoothhound.co.uk
Wales Travel Guide	www.britainexpress.com/wales
Welsh tourism websites	www.britfind.com/findwales.htm
Llandudno Tourism	www.llandudno-tourism.co.uk
Welsh Tourism Information	www.wales-calling.com
Brecon Beacons Tourism	www.brecon.co.uk
Pembrokshire Tourist Agency	www.pembrokeshire.co.uk
City of Swansea	www.swansea.com
Swansea, Mumbles and Gower Tourist Association	www.swansea-gower.demon.co.uk
Visitor Guide to North Wales & Cheshire	www.marl.com/lds
West and Wales Web	www.westwales.co.uk
Carmarthen County	www.carmarthencounty.co.uk
Guide to Snowdonia	www.snowdonia-wales.net
County of Monmouthshire	www.monmouthshire.org.uk
Beddgelert Tourism Association	www.beddgelerttourism.com
The village of Tegryn	www.tegryn.co.uk
The Town of Abergavenny	www.abergavenny.net

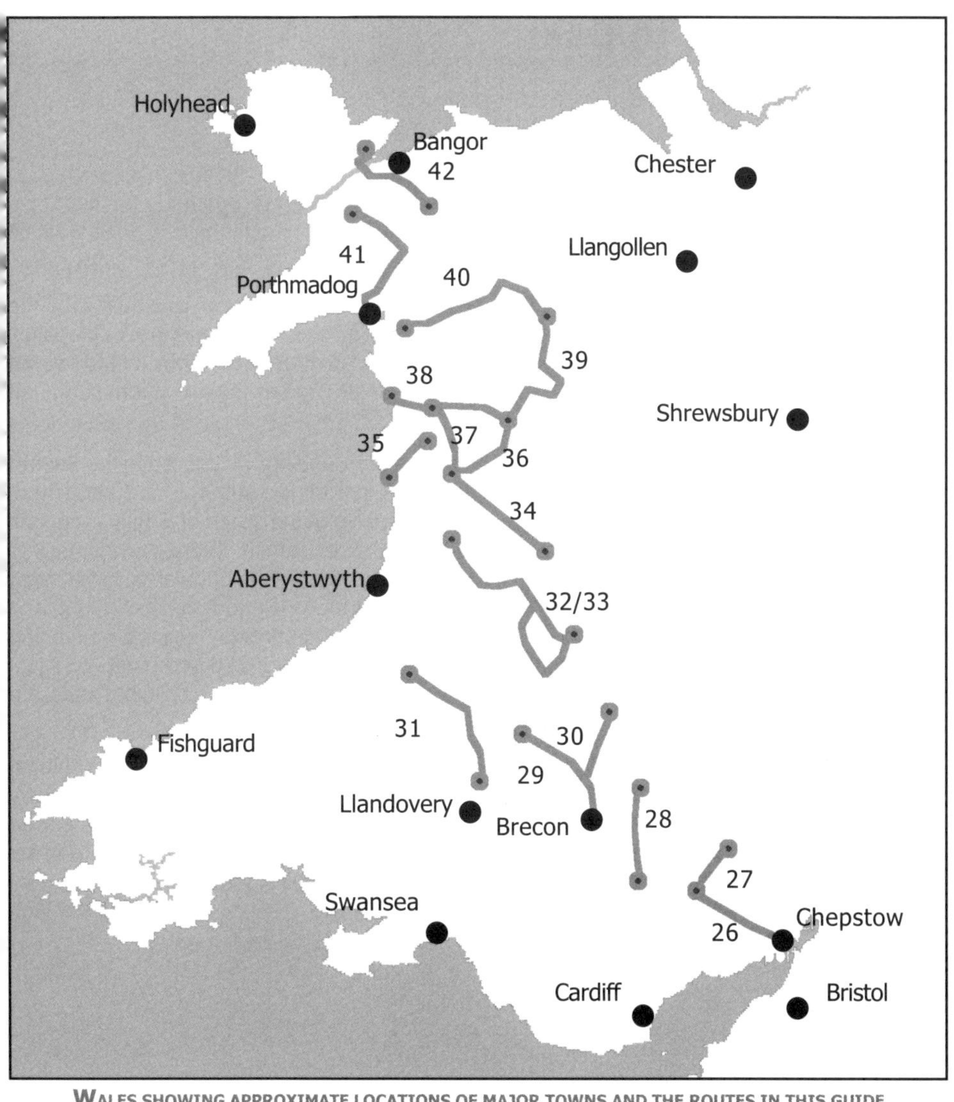

WALES SHOWING APPROXIMATE LOCATIONS OF MAJOR TOWNS AND THE ROUTES IN THIS GUIDE

26. Chepstow to Usk

Distance: **16.5 Miles**
Surface: **Good**
Scenery: **Rolling Countryside**

If you're coming into Wales from the south of England, then Chepstow is the first town you'll come to after crossing the Severn bridge on the M48. The temptation is to head west on the M4 and then strike north up into the centre of the country; but this is a much better way.

Leave the M48 motorway at junction 2 heading towards Chepstow, and then take the third exit at the roundabout, heading north on the A466. At the next roundabout Chepstow town centre is off to the right, but you should keep straight on and follow the signs for Monmouth for just under a mile. Then, as the roundabout with the B4293 comes into view, turn sharp left onto the B4235 towards Usk.

There's an immediate change in the road and the surroundings as you leave the Severn Valley behind and head off into the countryside. In an instant the suburbs and industry of Chepstow are behind you, the pressures and overcrowding of the south of England vanish, and it's as though you've crossed the boundary into another existence. There's an intimacy to everything that's hard to define, as the road twists and turns across the undulating landscape. This is a road that allows you to bond with your bike. The surface is good, the traffic light, and it's possible to make good progress. At the halfway point, the Carpenters Arms is a welcoming sight on the right as you skirt the edge of Shirenewton, but the road is so good that you'll just want to keep on going. Just give thanks to the geography of the low rolling hills that separate the Usk and Severn valleys.

Keep following the signs to Usk and cross over the main A449 road before beginning a descent into Usk town centre on the A472 Castle Parade. Usk is an old market town of busy narrow streets that lead down to the river, so if you're planning a break cross over the bridge to park up and then walk back into the centre for the shops, cafes and restaurants. There's a useful petrol station to the left on the far side of the bridge if you're getting low on fuel.

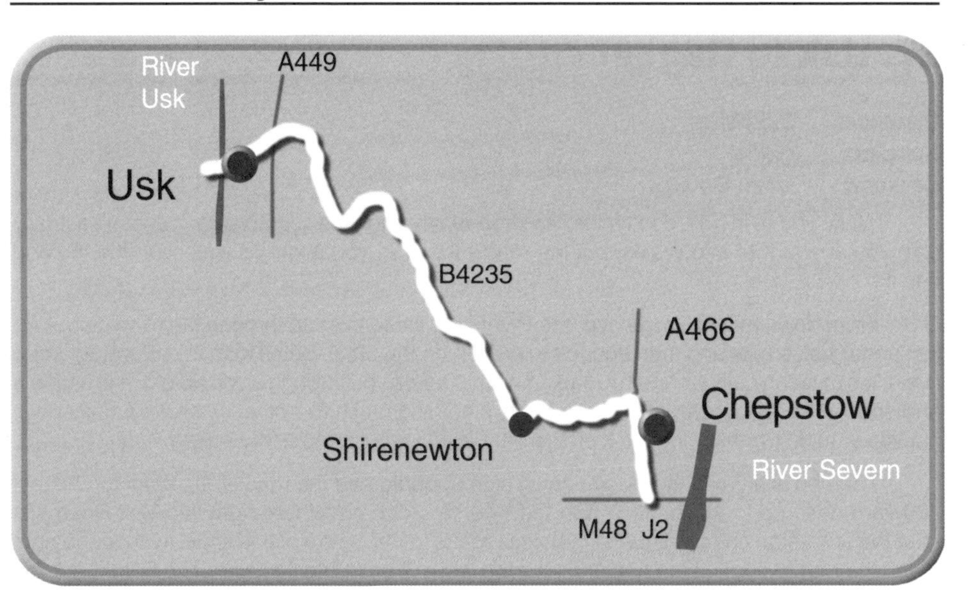

Road	Direction	Comment
A466	Chepstow	Leave M48 at J2 heading towards Chepstow and Monmouth at the roundabout
A466	Monmouth	Straight on at next roundabout towards Monmouth, and left on the B4235 before the next roundabout
B4235	Usk	Through Shirenewton and on to Usk

27. Usk to Raglan

Distance: 5.5 Miles
Surface: Good
Scenery: Open Country

While you're in Usk, don't miss this short run through the countryside. It doesn't actually take you any further into Wales, but the road's there so you might as well have the fun and ride it.

From down by the bridge over the River Usk, head east up through the town centre for just under half a mile and then bear off to the left on the Monmouth Road towards Raglan for five miles of technically wonderful road riding that takes you through a couple of small hamlets and ends at the quiet town of Raglan. There's nothing much to look at in the way of scenery, but you wouldn't want to look at it as the road itself is much more interesting.

The end is nigh as the Raglan town sign appears and the road straightens for the last 200 yard dash up to the junction with the A40. You can either turn right into Usk Road just after the town sign and continue to the cross roads in the centre of this small town, or go right round the roundabout on the A40 and take the last exit back into the town. The Beaufort Arms is in the centre of Raglan where these two roads meet, and is a good place for some refreshment before you ride all the way back to Usk.

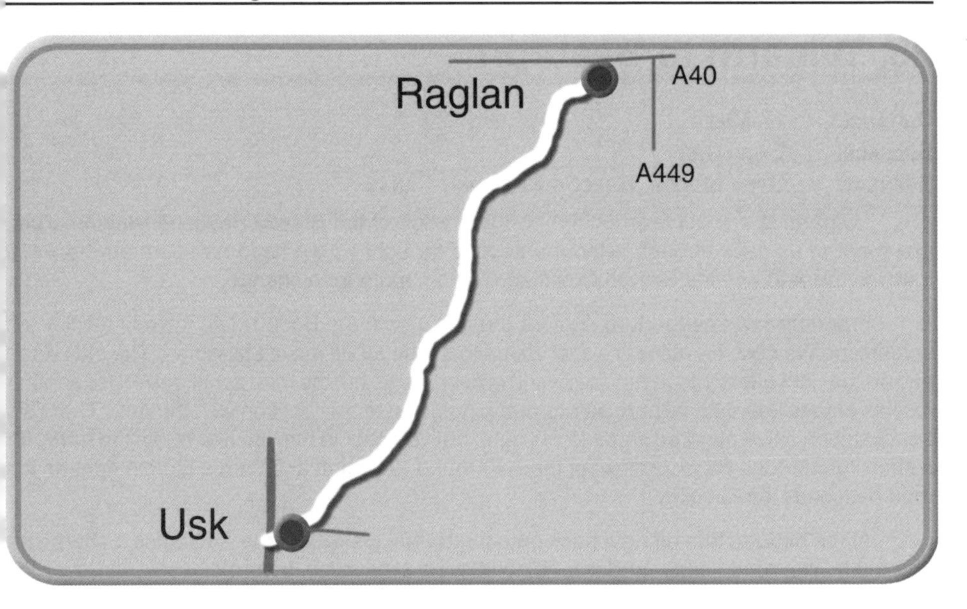

Road	Direction	Comment
No number	Usk Town Centre	From the bridge by the river head east through the town centre for about half a mile
No number	Raglan	Turn left onto Monmouth Road towards Raglan
No number	Raglan	Join the A40 - either go on to Raglan or turn round and come straight back

28. Talgarth to Beaufort

Distance: 17 Miles
Surface: Excellent
Scenery: Open Moors, Brecon Beacons, Canal

Talgarth is a small town on the northern edge of the Brecon Beacons National Park, that most of us pass through without a second thought as we head on south on the A479 towards the A40 and the Severn Crossing. Try this route for a change.

From the town centre turn right off the A479 onto the B4560. The town is quickly left behind and the next 4½ miles is a superb run to the small village of Llangorse. The old village pub on the right offers accommodation and refreshments but the road continues on for another 4 miles across the national park before dropping down to a T-junction with the A40. There's a petrol station a few hundred yards to the right, but you should turn left and rejoin the traffic for a short run through Bwlch, following the A40 round to the left and then a hairpin right as the road descends into a valley.

At the bottom, turn off right back onto the B4560 just where the A40 takes a sharp turn to the left. The road keeps on descending into the Usk valley, before crossing the over the river on a narrow bridge and then climbing up over the Brecon & Abergavenny Canal and into the village of Llangynidr.

The canal was built between 1797 and 1812 and once connected to the Monmouthshire Canal at Pontymoile. But now its 33 miles and 6 locks are completely isolated from the rest of the system. Used for the carriage of stone, coal and iron ore, the canal was served by an extensive network of tramways that bought these raw materials down from the hills for transhipment into the barges. Many of the trackways can still be seen and some of the wharves still have the old rails in place.

There's another petrol station in Llangynidr on the left, just before the T-junction, where you should turn left onto the B4558 for half a mile before turning right back onto the B4560 again for Beaufort and Tredegar.

The road now twists and turns and climbs steeply on to open moorland that's a popular place for day trips and picnics at the weekend. The views back across the national park are superb, and in marked contrast to the view ahead as you drop off the plateau into a valley that was once part of the thriving Welsh coal and steel industry. The final 1½ miles to Beaufort and the T-junction with the A465 Heads of the Valleys road has little to commend it.

Moorland above Beaufort

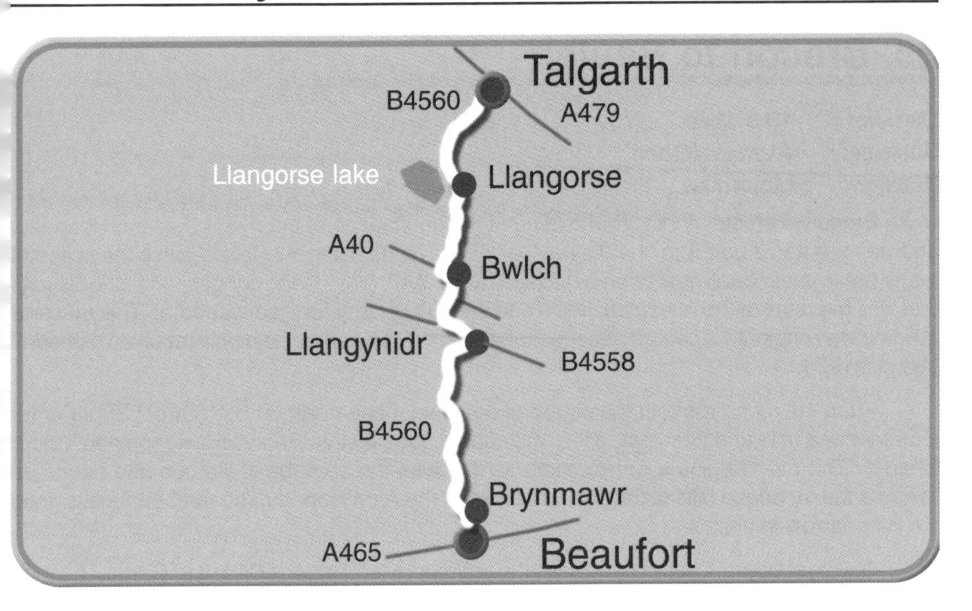

Road	Direction	Comment
A479		From town centre take the A479 and take the right turn onto the B4560
B4560	Llangorse Bwlch	Follow theB4560 until it meets the A40
A40		Turn left, through Bwlch and then turn right back onto the B4560
B4560	Llangynidr	Turn left at junction onto B4558
B4558		Turn right after half a mile back onto the B4560
B4560	Beaufort	Follow the road to Brynmawr and Beaufort

29. Brecon to Beulah

Distance: 19.5 Miles
Surface: Average/Good
Scenery: Mountains

Brecon is an old market town sitting at the confluence of the rivers Usk and Honddhu, and was granted a borough charter way back in 1270. The narrow streets, once the scene of many traffic jams, have now been bypassed by the A40, leaving the congestion to the tourists that visit the ruins of the medieval castle and the 13th century fortified cathedral. This massive building was originally a church attached to the Benedictine priory, and only received cathedral status in1923.

From the roundabout in the centre of the town, head north on High Street Superior for a quarter of a mile and then just before the church, turn left into Priory Hill, signposted 'Upper Chapel'. The road begins a gentle climb as it leaves the suburbs of Brecon and heads up towards the moorland hills following the course of the Afon Honddu.The road surface is good if a little narrow in places.

Just past Upper Chapel don't miss the sharp turn left onto the B4519 to Garth. The road soon crosses a cattle grid, narrows a little more, and then moves out onto the open moorland whilst twisting and bumping its way around the edge of the hills. There are a lot of blind corners along this stretch, all the drops are unprotected, and a large number of the sheep grazing on this land seem to belong to the Welsh Suicidal Sheep Racing Team! So just take things a little steady and enjoy the magnificent views across the Mynydd Eppynt.

Pen y Fan - the 2,906 ft summit of the Brecon Beacons

Once over the mountain range, the road begins a descent into the valley of the River Irfon and some of the bends are a little on the tight side. As the road enters Garth it passes under the railway line, and at the T-junction with the A483 you should turn left towards Llanwrytd Wells and Llandovery.

After the rigours of the mountain it's a relief to find that the A483 is a wide well surfaced piece of road that takes you to the small village of Beulah three miles away, where there's a pub and restaurant on the right that makes a useful break. There's a petrol station here as well.

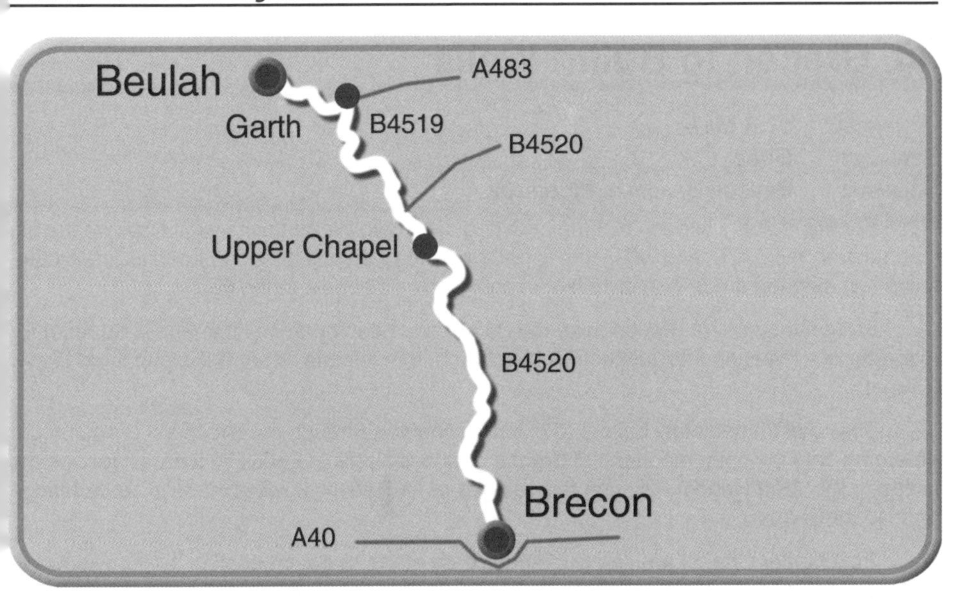

Road	Direction	Comment
B4520	High St Superior	Head north from the centre of town onto High Street Superior
B4520	Upper Chapel	Turn left into Priory Hill
B4519	Garth	Sharp left turn just outside Upper Chapel onto the B4519
A483	Beulah	Left on the A483 towards Llanwrytd and Llandovery

30. Brecon to Builth Wells

Distance: **17.5 Miles**
Surface: **Good**
Scenery: **Brecon Beacons, Moorland**

For the majority of people, a trip between these two Welsh towns would involve the big loop east on the A470, and while this is not a bad road there's a much better, shorter route, that's just as good a ride with excellent scenery and it's almost traffic-free to boot!

From the centre of Brecon, take the B4520 and head north on High Street Superior for a quarter of a mile and then just before the church, turn left into Priory Hill, signposted Upper Chapel.

The road immediately begins to climb, taking you through the Brecon suburbs before emerging onto the open moorland of Brecon Beacons National Park. From here it follows the valley of the Afon Honddu through the villages of Pwllgloyw, Lower Chapel, Castle Madoc and Upper Chapel.

Past Upper Chapel and the good ride really starts to get interesting as the wide well-surfaced road sweeps and swoops over the Mynydd Eppynt and around the edge of a restricted military area, which probably explains its quality. There's some wild and barren countryside here, but when the sun shines the views are superb. However when it's raining and the wind's blowing, it's one of the most lonesome places on the planet.

Enjoy this by-product of MoD spending, and the lack of military or any other traffic, and have a cracking ride all the way down into Builth Wells, where the road joins the A470 and the A483.

The B4520 near Upper Chapel

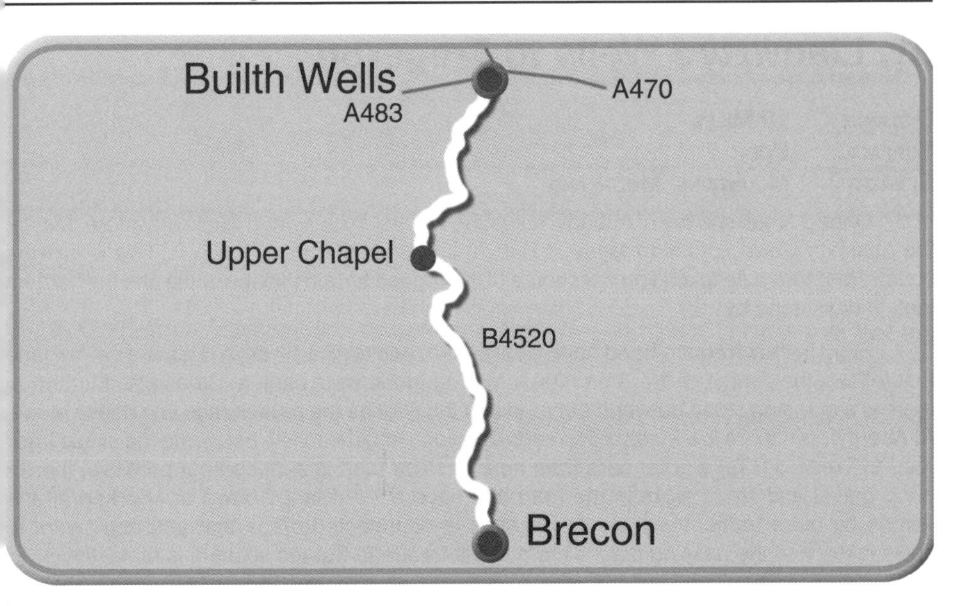

Road	Direction	Comment
B4520	High St Superior	Head north from the centre of town onto High Street Superior
B4520	Upper Chapel	Turn left into Priory Hill
B4520	Builth Wells	Continue through Upper Chapel all the way to Builth Wells

31. Llanwrtyd Wells to Tregaron

Distance: **18 Miles**
Surface: **Poor**
Scenery: **Mountains, Moorland**

Once a small spa town, nobody 'takes the waters' in Llanwrtyd Wells any more. Maybe the desolate views across to Mynydd Eppynt had something to do with it. This is drovers country and the route takes you over some of the rugged terrain that the cattle and the herders took in days gone by.

From the town centre head north west on the road to Abergwesyn. This is a narrow lane that follows the course of the Afon Irfon, crossing to the west bank at Dinas Mill. Further on there is a standing stone between the road and the river as the route heads into dense forest. At Abergwesyn there is a small crossroads and you should turn left here onto the single track road to Tregaron. Take great care from here on. The road is surfaced but primitive, there's often gravel and small rocks in the road that have been washed down or knocked off the verges by other traffic, there are some serious unprotected drops that you don't want to investigate, and the passing places are not that frequent. But the scenery is fantastic!

After following the river for a couple of miles, the road crosses a small bridge that has only recently replaced a ford, and climbs steeply into the Tywi Forest. There are two narrow hairpin bends here with a 1 in 4 gradient, so be extremely careful. If it's rained within the last week the surface will also be wet and slippery. The ridge is narrow and almost immediately the road drops steeply into a small moorland valley, and then just as quickly climbs back out again. After skirting the knoll of Esgair Gelli, it's another steep descent into Nant-y-Maen, a narrow river crossing, and a climb out the other side. Before the bridge there's a track off to the right which takes you to a bleak moorland area of cairns and standing stones, but only try this on foot!

In the Irfon Valley

Past Esgair Ffrwd the road goes back into forestry and the contour-hopping settles down a bit as the road picks up on the Afon Berwyn, and generally follows the course of the river valley all the way down to Tregaron. As you enter the town there's a carpark on the left with public toilets, but if you don't 'feel the need' then carry on for a hundred yards or so to the town square, where there's plenty of space to park as you'll probably need a rest after the journey. Tregaron is an old but quiet market town, so there's shops and pubs to hand.

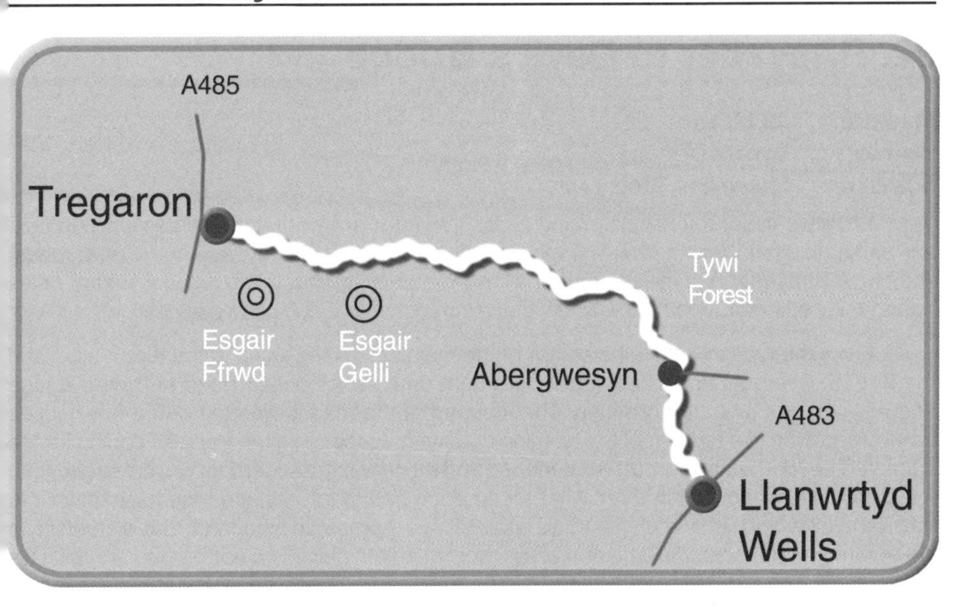

Road	Direction	Comment
No number	Abergwesyn	Head north west out of the town centre on a narrow lane towards Abergwesyn
No number	Abergwesyn	At Abergwesyn turn left towards Tregaron
No number	Tregaron	Follow the narrow road to Tregaron. Be careful of gravel and rocks in the road
		At Tregaron there is a car park

32. Rhayader to Devil's Bridge

Distance: **29 Miles**
Surface: **Average/Poor**
Scenery: **Mountains, Moorland**

With two major roads converging on it, Rhayader is a bit of a mid-Wales junction box, and although other Welsh towns and villages have managed to get bypasses and relief roads, somehow Rhayader has missed out on all this road construction. The result is that at times during busy summer months the whole place can come to a complete standstill.

From the crossroads in the centre of the town, follow the signs to the Elan Valley and the B4518. After just under half-a-mile turn right onto the Mountain Road to Devil's Bridge and Aberystwyth and start climbing. The first part of the road is wooded with a few houses around and then you're clear of the tree line and out onto the open moors, still heading for the summit. The road is narrow but well surfaced and the views are superb as you cross over into the upper valley of the Afon Elan. After the junction on the left with the road back down into the Elan Valley and Rhayader, the route takes off over some wild moorland, that is stunning in the summer months but must be one of the most desolate places on earth in the winter. This is serious sheep farming country (what else would live up here!), so look out for those white woolly things getting caught up in the spokes, especially around Easter and the lambing season.

The road is narrow and unfenced now almost all the way to Cwmystwyth, and there's some old mine workings on the right just before you get there, where the road runs alongside the Afon Ystwyth. Past Cwmystwyth, the road climbs and you should take the right fork for the B4574 to Devil's Bridge. The road runs through forestry before dropping steeply down to a T-junction with the A4120. Turn left and almost immediately park up on the right opposite the hotel. If the bar's not open, then there's an excellent tea room where you can take a well-earned break. If you're up to it, then you can take a stroll down to the Devil's Bridge itself. This 12th century structure is the lowest of three bridges built close together over the Afon Mynach, where it meets the Afon Rheidol in a series of spectacular waterfalls. The highest of these is 300 ft.

An alternative route to the mountain road is to go around the Elan Valley Reservoirs - see route 33.

On the Mountain Road - look out for woolly jumpers

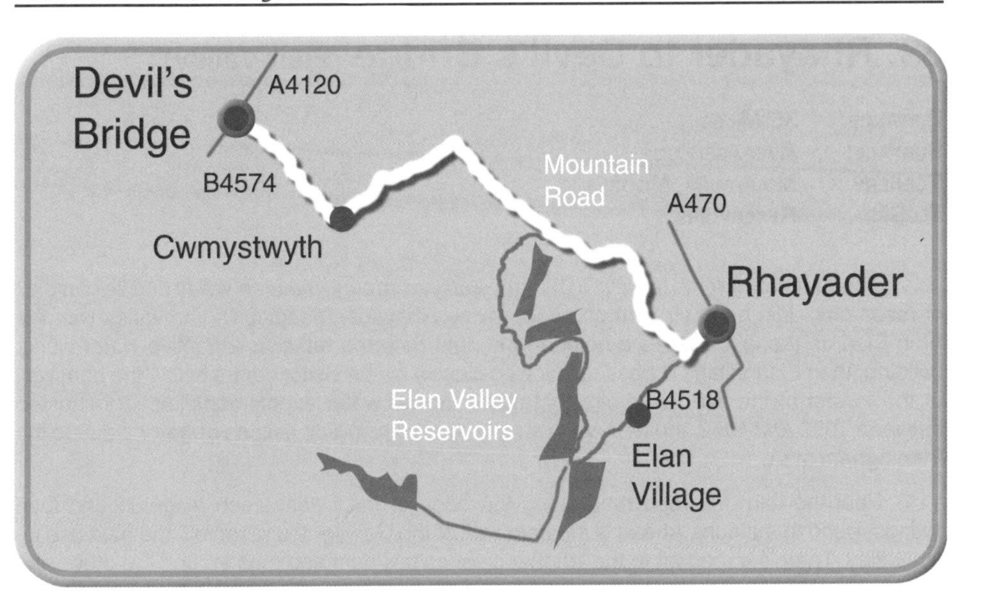

Road	Direction	Comment
B4518	Elan Valley	Turn right after half a mile on to the Mountain Road *(or go straight on for the Elan Valley, Route 33)*
No number	Devil's Bridge	Keep straight on at junction or turn left to go back to Elan Valley
No number	Cwmystwyth	Take right fork past Cwmystwyth onto the B4574
B4574	Devil's Bridge	Left at the junction with the A4120 for cafe and hotel

(Elan Valley, Route 33 can be done on the way back, in which case turn right at the junction and go down to the Elan Valley)

33. Rhayader to Devil's Bridge (Elan Valley)

Distance: 35 Miles
Surface: Average/Poor
Scenery: Mountains, Moorland
To See: Reservoirs

This alternative route to Devil's Bridge takes you through the Elan Valley and its complex of reservoirs. Just head straight on after leaving Rhayader, heading up the valley with the Afon Elan on the left. There's a hotel on the right before a rather unattractive water works building, then Elan Village is passed followed closely by the visitor centre below the dam wall of the lowest of the five reservoirs that make up the water supply complex. Constructed between 1892 and 1952, the reservoirs supply over sixty million gallons of water a day to the Birmingham area.

Past the dam the road runs along the edge of the Caban-coch reservoir and then swings round to the right. Ahead is the dam wall of the Garreg-ddu reservoir, the next one up the valley. There's a road off to the left that crosses this dam and runs around the other side of Caban-coch. This will take you up a side valley to the Caerwen reservoir, the biggest of the group. The views across the lake are spectacular and it's well worth the trip.

Continuing alongside Garreg-ddu, the road rises and then drops down again to the head of the valley, where it turns sharp left and crosses a bridge before doing a hairpin right and climbing up to the next dam at the base of the Penygarreg reservoir. There's a small lay-by here on the right and it's worth a brief stop for the view. The road runs on along the lakeside until the valley turns sharp right. Here, the road executes a hairpin across a side-stream and runs across moorland before rejoining the waters edge at the dam that separates it from Craig Goch, the fifth and highest reservoir.

Turn right here and cross the dam for a parking area, benches and toilets. Carry straight on and it's open moorland with the reservoir below and to the right all the way to the Pont ar Elan, where the road crosses the Afon Elan again and climbs up to a T-junction with the Mountain Road. Turn right here for a 17 mile circular trip back to Rhayader, and left for Devil's Bridge. (See route 32)

Craig Goch Reservoir

One word of warning; despite the narrowness of the road, forty seater coaches use the route up the Elan Valley. They are not nice things to meet head-on around a blind bend!

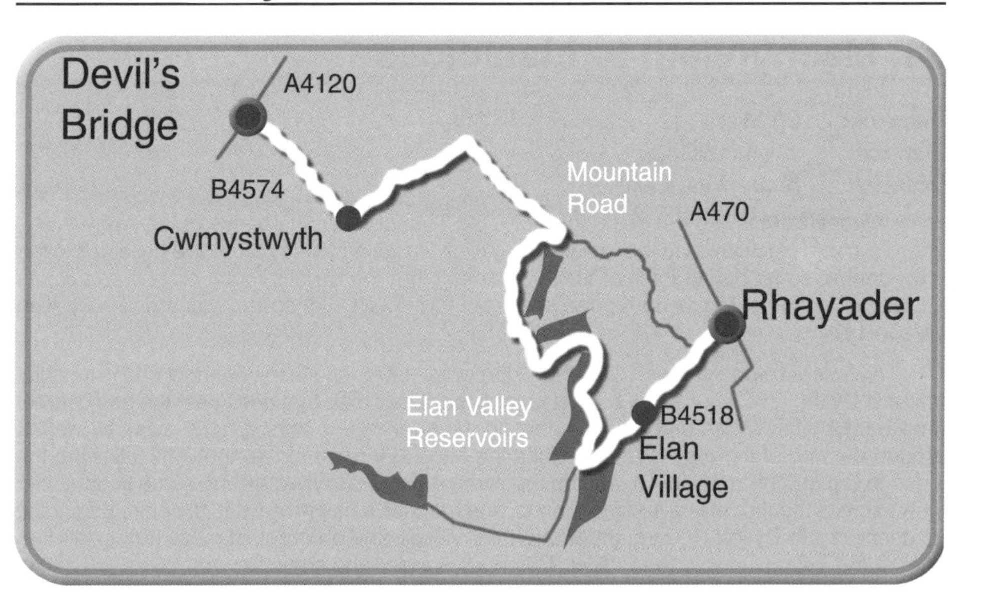

Road	Direction	Comment
B4518	Elan Valley	Keep on past Elan village and swing round to the right past the dam.
Unmarked	Elan Valley	Keep on the road until it meets up with the Mountain Road and turn left for Cwmystwyth
Unmarked	Cwmystwyth	Take right fork past Cwmystwyth onto the B4574
B4574	Devil's Bridge	Left at junction with the A4120 for cafe and hotel

34. Machynlleth to Llanidloes

DISTANCE: **20 MILES**
SURFACE: **AVERAGE/GOOD**
SCENERY: **MOUNTAINS, LAKES**

Machynlleth is laid out in the form of a big T-junction on the banks of the river Dovey. There's an old clock tower in the middle of the High Street and many attractive buildings in the town centre, some dating back to the 17th century, but the town is much older than this, as there was settlement here during the Iron Age and Owen Glendower was proclaimed king here in 1404.

Head east along the High Street past the clock tower, and then bear right by the hospital towards Dylife. This is a narrow but reasonably surfaced road that goes past the golf course, crosses the Afon Dulas and then runs along the river valley. After it turns away to the left around the end of the mountain spur, take the second turn off to the right, still following the signs to Dylife. The road now heads up the flank of Esgair Graflwyn giving some spectacular views across the mountains and moorlands, and reaches a height of 1,650 ft. before beginning its descent into Dylife. Go straight through the village and a couple of miles further on turn right at the T-junction with the B4518. This road is wider and smoother and takes you all the way into Llanidloes.

Past the village of Staylittle, and the road really takes off in a series of sweeps, dips and crests before the flooded valley of Llyn Clywedog appears on the right and the road drops down alongside the lake and crosses an earth embankment that closes off an arm of the valley. There's a car park here and public toilets! A couple of miles further on there's a turn off to the right that will take you right up to the dam wall. There's also a cafe up here, and the remains of the old Bryn Tail Lead Mines down on the valley floor.

Lead mining was a major industry around here in the 19th century, although Bryn Tail was never a big producer with a highest recorded output of 384 tons in 1851. Ten years later it became part of the larger Van Consols Mining Company and production switched to barytes (white lead), but by 1884 it all got too much and the mine finally closed. Llyn Clywedog was constructed in the 1960s to maintain the flow of water in the River Severn during periods of low rainfall. The concrete buttress dam is over 235 feet high and holds 11,000 million gallons.

Back on the B4518 and a few miles further on you'll reach the outskirts Llanidloes. There's a roundabout here with a welcoming petrol station off to the left, and if you turn right the road will take you into the centre of this small town.

LLYN CLYWEDOGG AND THE LEAD ORE WORKINGS

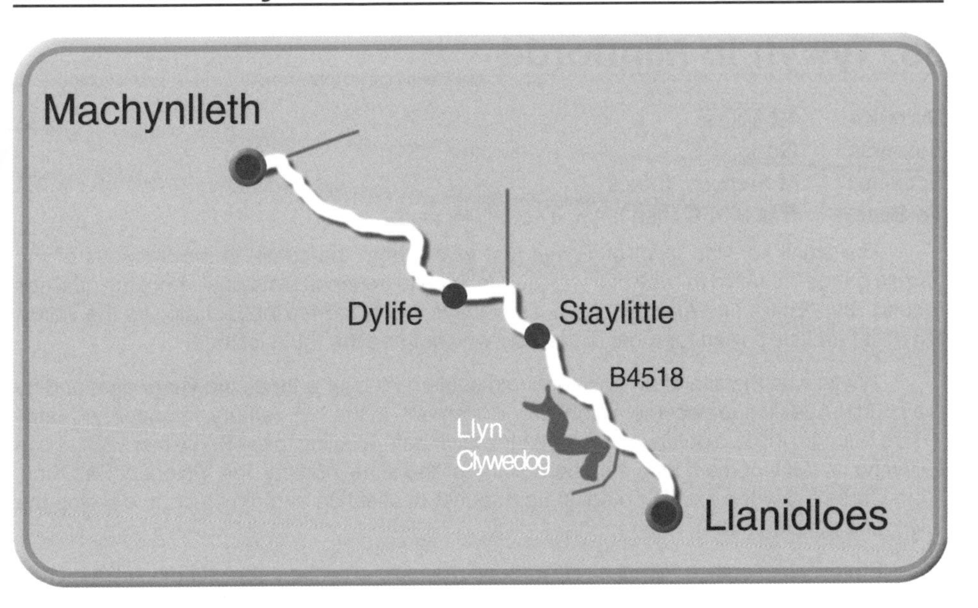

Road	Direction	Comment
A489	East	Head east along the High Street past the clock tower
Unmarked	Dylife	At hospital bear right
Unmarked	Dylife	Take the second right after the end of the mountain spur
Unmarked	Dylife	Through Dylife and turn right onto the B4518
B4518	Llanidloes	Past Staylittle to Llanidloes. Take the turn to right about two miles past the lake to go to the dam wall and a cafe (which never seems to be open) or carry on to Llanidloes

35. Tywyn to Minffordd

Distance: 12 Miles
Surface: Good
Scenery: Mountains, Lakes
To See: Railway, Cader Idris, Tal-y-llyn lake

The small seaside town of Tywyn just inland from the coast, is the terminus of the narrow gauge Tal-y-llyn railway that was built in 1865 to transport slate down from the quarries around Bryn-Eglws and Abergynolwyn. Nowadays it only carries tourist traffic up the valley, but as it parallels a road for most of the way why not ride the route instead.

Tywyn was the site of an ancient Druid settlement over a thousand years ago, and by the Middle Ages it had become a Christian settlement. In the 13th century, the nearby Castell y Bere became the last defence of Prince Llewellyn before falling to the English in 1231. Then following its development as a shipment point for the slate industry, the Victorian 'Salt King' John Corbett saw the town's potential as a tourist destination and did much to develop the town as a seaside resort.

From Tywyn station take the A493 inland, heading past the petrol station to Bryn-crug. Turn right here on to the B4405 and follow this road as it almost immediately turns left and heads off up one side of the valley with the railway line on the other. The valley narrows as the road and the railway approach Dolgoch, and the road makes sharp 90 degree right and left turns to run past the Dolgoch Falls station.

From the station the road and the railway run close together all the way up the still narrowing valley to Abergynolwyn where the railway finishes, but the original line headed up into the mountains and the old slate quarries. There's a slate museum here.

The road continues straight on with a few twists and turns, crossing back to the north side of the valley again and following the Afon Dysynni to the Tal-y-llyn lake. Sitting here by the lakeside on a warm summer's evening with the peak of Cader Idris reflecting from the still surface of the lake is one of life's moments. Doing it outside the Pen-y-bont Hotel with a cold beer in your hand makes the moment even better! But I digress.

Continuing on, the road runs right along the southeastern edge of the mile-long lake, following nearly every twist and turn of the shoreline before it joins the A487 at Minffordd. Turn right here for Corris and Machynlleth, or left for Dolgellau.

Tal-y-Llyn Railway

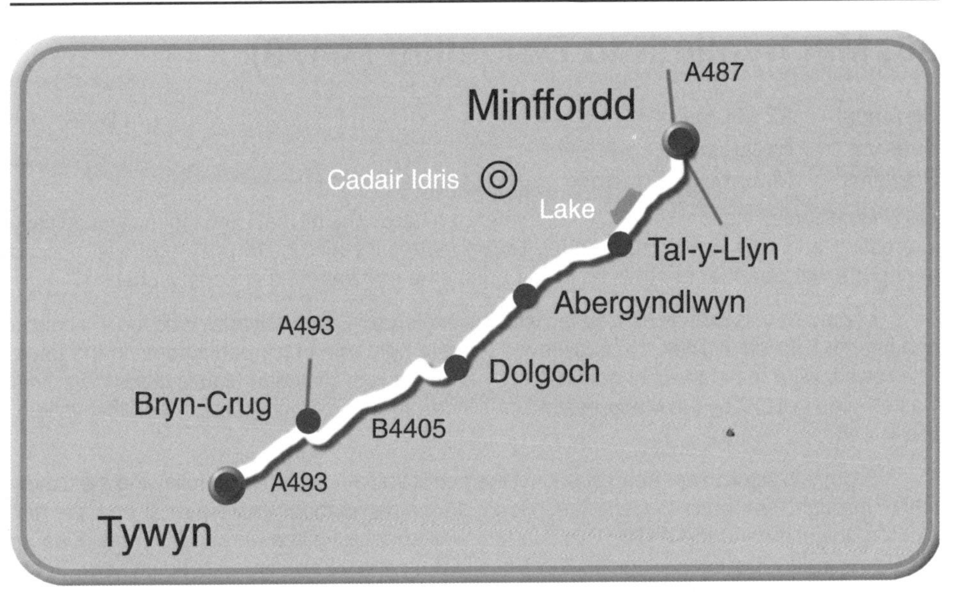

Road	Direction	Comment
A493	Bryn-Crug	From Tywyn Station take the A493 to Bryn-Crug
B4405	Dolgoch	Turn right onto the B4405 and follow it all the way to Minffordd
A487		At Minffordd join the A487 and turn left for Dolgellau or right for Corris or Machynlleth

36. Machynlleth to Dolgellau (A470)

Distance: 22 Miles
Surface: Excellent
Scenery: Mountains, Forests

I just couldn't ignore the A470 completely, so here's the bit that I find the most scenically interesting and technically challenging. Unfortunately it's also quite busy and well policed during the warmer drier months, so pick a quiet time and keep the speeds in check.

Machynlleth is closely associated with the exploits of Owain Glyndwr who led a rebellion against the English in 1404. He is believed to have held one of his parliaments in the town. The town's wide main street is dominated by an elaborate Victorian Gothic clock tower that was erected in 1873 by the Marquess of Londonderry, whose family home, Plas Machynlleth, lies in parkland nearby.

From this clock tower head east past the petrol station on the A489, following the Dovey valley through Penegoes to Cemmaes Road. At the roundabout (more petrol) take the first exit for Dolgellau and the A470. This is a fast well-surfaced piece of road that continues up the Dovey valley, but keep it legal as the 'Boys In Blue' are usually around somewhere. To the left are the wooded slopes of the Dovey Forest, the downfall of many an aspiring rally driver; whilst on the right are the barren slopes of Mynydd y Cemais and the 1,500 ft. peak of Esgair Ddu.

At Mallwyd there's a roundabout at the junction with the A458 and a petrol station which also doubles as the village stores. Continue on the A470 through Minllyn and past Dinas Mawddwy (try the Red Lion Inn for good food, drink and accommodation), where the road starts to climb up into the mountains again. This is an excellent piece of road, but look out for the sharp right-hander over a blind crest at Ochr-y-Bwlch. It's caught out quite a few people - myself included!

From here the road continues over the mountains before dropping down to the Cross Foxes Inn (good food) where the B4405 Tywyn road joins from the left as the road sweeps round to the right. The scenery is wooded from here on, and after a few straight sections, the road descends the Afon Wnion valley into Dolgellau through a number of sweeping curves. Just after the Esso petrol station on the right, turn left into Aran Road and follow this road past the Clifton House Hotel as it curves right through the town centre to the bridge over the Afon Wnion. There's plenty of parking here.

Dolgellau is a small market town that began life as a village in the 12th century and developed from its central role in the county's woollen industry. This reached its peak around 1800, but declined over the following century due to the introduction of mechanical mills. During production, the wool was transported down the River Wnion, then along the Mawddach before ending up in the port of Barmouth about 10 miles away. From here it was shipped all around the world. The Welsh gold rush of the 19th century was centred on the area and T.H. Roberts Ironmongers was an important source of panning equipment to the 500 miners who worked in the gold and copper mines in the hills around the town towards the end of the century.

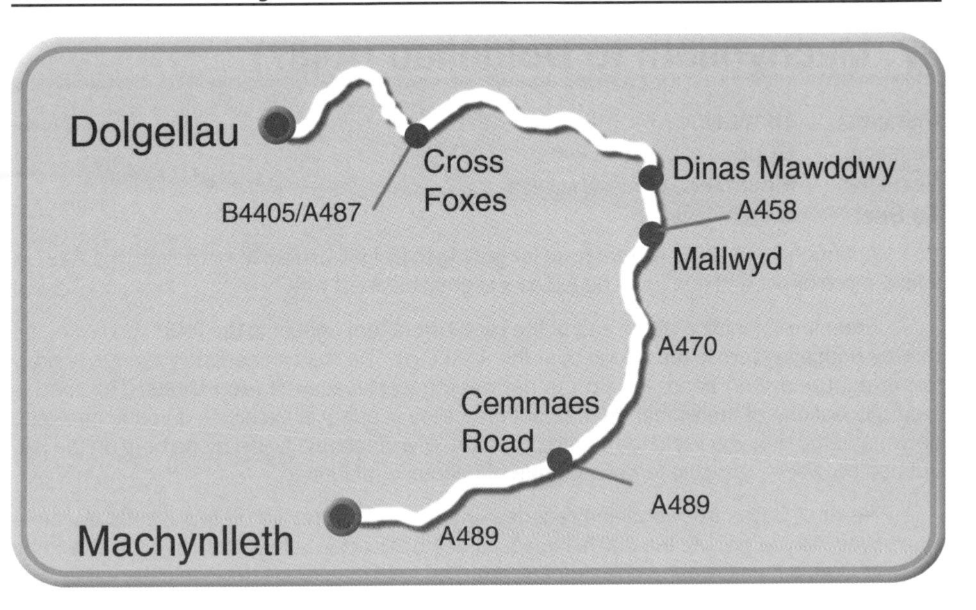

Road	Direction	Comment
A489	Cemmaes Road	Head east from the clock tower to the roundabout at Cemmaes Road
A470	Dolgellau	Continue on the A470 at the roundabout at Mallwyd
A470	Dolgellau	Turn left into Aran Road at Dolgellau for the town centre

37. Machynlleth to Dolgellau (A487)

DISTANCE: 16 MILES
SURFACE: GOOD
SCENERY: MOUNTAINS, LAKES/VALLEYS
TO SEE: CADAIR IDRIS

Although the A470 is a great road for getting to Dolgellau from Machynlleth, the A487 is a little more direct and just as good but in a slightly different way.

From the T-junction at the end of the High Street turn right onto the A487, go under the railway bridge and cross the bridge over the Afon Dyfi. The road immediately swings sharply to the right and then bears left up the narrow forrested valley of Afon Dinas. The road is naturally not one of the widest around, but the valley scenery is excellent. If you're into wind power and the like, you'll find the Centre for Alternative Technology just along here on the left, but don't expect to be able to get a couple of gallons of unleaded.

North of Corris the woodland recedes and the road turns left up and climbs up into a side valley. As you go over the 660 ft. high pass at the top of the valley, you'll see the awesome mass of Cadair Idris towering up in front of you. The road then drops down into the valley, and at Minffordd the road from Tywyn joins from the left. The A487 continues to climb along the valley floor through some incredibly rugged mountain scenery. The road is straight and smooth here, but there's a few kinks and bumps just waiting to catch out the unwary on the climb up to the summit pass at 926 ft. The road drops quickly down the other side through sweeping curves before making a beeline for the T-junction with the A470 by the Cross Foxes Inn. Turn left here and follow the road as it sweeps down into the valley of the Afon Wnion and Dolgellau.

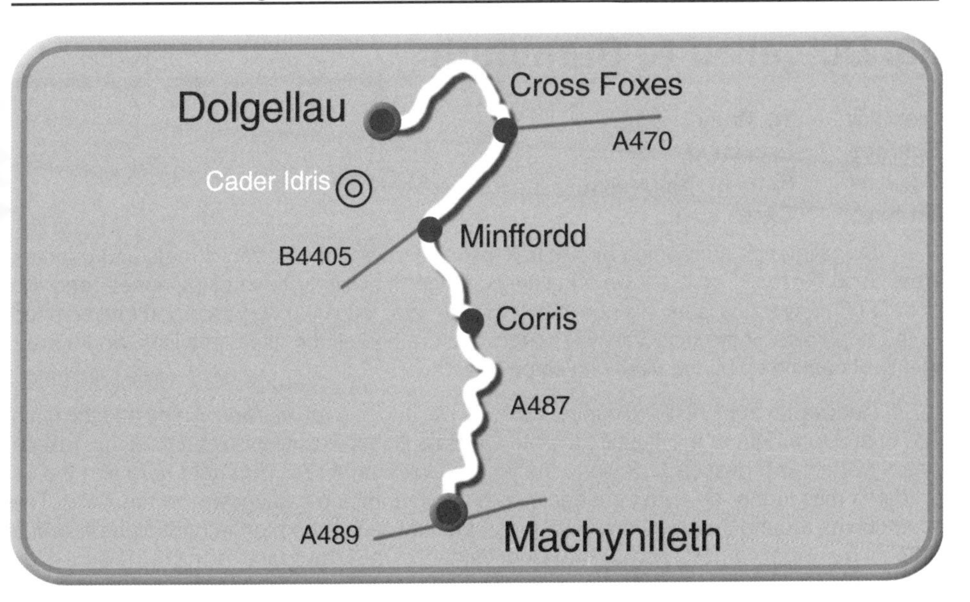

Road	Direction	Comment
A487	Dolgellau	Turn onto A487 from T-junction at end of the High Street
A487	Dolgellau	Straight on at Minffordd
A470	Dolgellau	Turn left at the junction with the A470

38. Dolgellau to Barmouth

Distance: 10 Miles
Surface: Excellent
Scenery: Estuary, Mountains
To See: Cader Idris

Dolgellau has a brooding air about it, possibly due to the narrow streets and the dark slate used for many of the town's buildings. Once the county town of Merioneth and the source of many traffic jams, it's now much quieter after the A470 was enlarged and diverted to the north side of the river valley. The town centre has all the usual services, and there's plenty of parking up by the river with cafes close by.

Head north from the town centre, crossing the bridge over the Afon Wnion and the main A470, and turn right at the T-junction onto the Bala Road. Follow this road past the Texaco petrol station as it descends down to the junction with the A494. Turn right here and then a third of a mile further on, turn right again onto the northbound carriageway of the A470. The road curves around the town in a cutting and then sweeps round to the right along a raised embankment that carries it across the upper estuary of the Mawddach river. On the north side of the river turn left towards Barmouth on the A496. This is a lovely smooth quick road that snakes along the base of the hills that run right down to the river's edge, with spectacular views across the estuary to the mountains of the Cader Idris range. Two miles from Barmouth, the road narrows dramatically as it is squeezed into the diminishing gap between the encroaching mountains and the water's edge. There's a petrol station on the edge of Barmouth, but it's a bit pricey so you'd have been better off filling up in Dolgellau. Turn left under the railway bridge and find somewhere to park up down by the lifeboat station.

Barmouth is a seaside resort that's looking a bit faded and run down these days, but there'll be no problems getting refreshments, a stick of rock . . . or candy floss . . . or a bucket and spade! And if you've brought your rod and line with you, then there's good fishing for mullet, mackerel and sea bass around here.

As an alternative you could head out of Dolgellau on the A493 towards Tywyn, and at Penmaenpool turn right and take the toll road across the estuary and the recently rebuilt river bridge to the north shore. Then turn left on the A496 and head off to Barmouth.

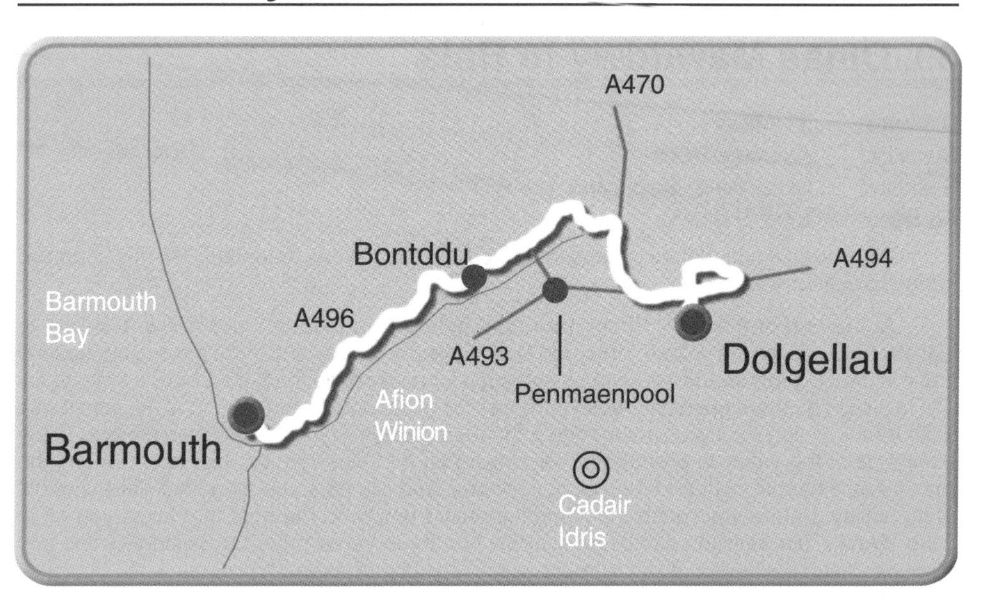

Road	Direction	Comment
Town Centre	North	From the town centre head north over the bridge.
Bala Road		Turn right at the T-junction onto Bala Rd
A494		Turn right at the junction with the A494
A470	Trawsfynydd Ffestiniog	Turn right onto the A470
A496	Barmouth	Turn left onto the A496 and follow it all the way to Barmouth *(As an alternative you can head west out of Dolgellau on the A493 to Penmaenpool and then turn right to Barmouth over the toll bridge)*

39. Dinas Mawddwy to Bala

DISTANCE: 31 MILES
SURFACE: AVERAGE/POOR
SCENERY: MOUNTAINS, MOORLAND
TO SEE: LAKE VYRNWY

Dinas is now completely bypassed by the A470, which has fortunately left this attractive village largely unspoilt.

At the end of the High Street, turn right by the Red Lion Inn and follow this road to Llanymaddwy along the valley of the Afon Dyfi. It's pretty narrow and there's some agricultural traffic in the neighbourhood, so keep an eye open for mud on the road. It's a bit of a switchback ride in places as there obviously wasn't any earth moving equipment around at the time it was built. After passing through Llanymaddwy, the road passes Bryn Hall and then crosses to the other side of the valley in preparation for striking off for Lake Vyrnwy. Just past Penant, the road takes a hairpin right and then climbs, climbs, and climbs some more in order to get out of the valley. Before you reach the summit there's the turn to the right that takes you off to Lake Vyrnwy, but keep on climbing for a few hundreds yards more up Bwlch-y-Groes and there's a magnificent view north from the summit pass across to Snowdonia.

Return back down and take the turn to the lake that's now on the left, go across the cattle grid that marks the boundary of the National Park, and follow this narrow undulating road/track across the moorland and down to the lakeside. At the T-junction turn right and follow the road around the shoreline. The surface is a bit rough in patches, it's narrow, and it stays wet long after the rain has stopped as the trees overhang the road in many places. A mile or so along the road there's a large picnic area on the lakeside, complete with a most unusual insect sculpture and more importantly a (small) public toilet. At the end of the lake just past the dam, there's a useful coffee shop and a not-so-useful souvenir shop. If you're feeling energetic then you can swap horsepower for pedal power and rent a mountain bike.

Lake Vyrnwy was formed in 1881 when the valley was flooded to make a reservoir to supply drinking water to Liverpool. At five miles in length and nearly one mile wide, it's the largest man-made lake in Wales. Take the road across the dam wall and head back up the other side of the lake, past the pump house where the water is extracted, and all the way up to the head of the valley. There's a road off to the right here to Bala, so unless you want to keep going round and round the lake, you'd be advised to turn right.

THE VIEW FROM BWLCH-Y-GROES

The road climbs away from the lake following the valley of the Afon Nadroedd, and then strikes off across the moorland watershed before finding the valley of Afon Hirnant to take it down to Bala. The road runs through forest following the descent of the river, and on lower ground it crosses a small bridge and turns to the right. Keep following the signs to Bala, turning left at the next junction and then left again at the junction with the B4391. Follow this road for a mile to the crossroads with the A494. Turn left here and the centre of Bala is a few hundred yards down the road.

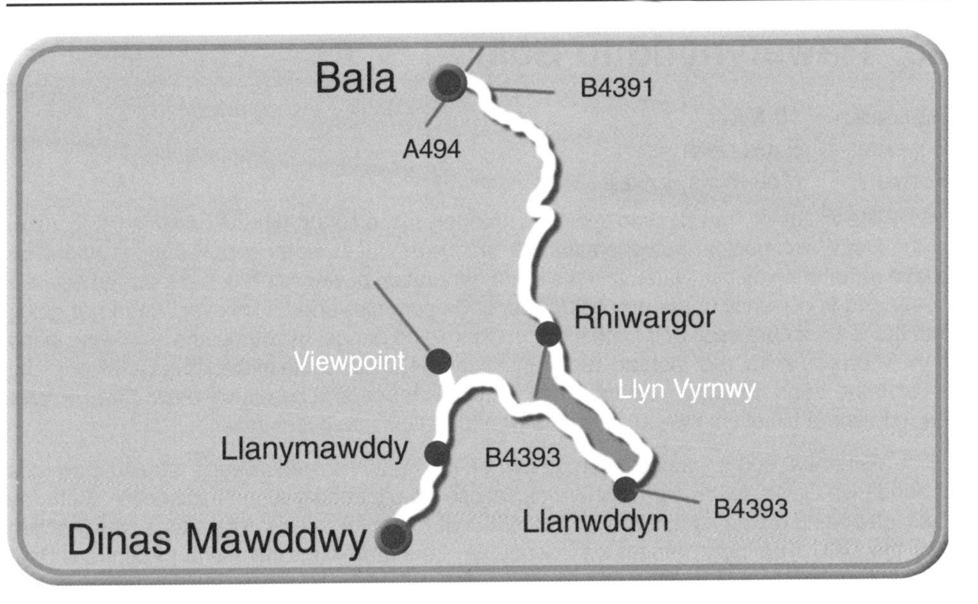

Road	Direction	Comment
High St		Turn right by the Red Lion Inn
Unmarked	Llanymawddy	Straight on for viewpoint. Turn right for Llyn Vyrnwy
B4393	Llanwddyn	Right at the T-junction and follow the road around the lake
Unmarked	Bala	Turn right for Bala
Unmarked	Bala	Turn left at the first junction
B4391	Bala	Turn left at the junction with the B4391
A494	Bala	Turn left onto the A494 to the centre of Bala

40. Trawsfynydd to Bala

DISTANCE: **18 MILES**
SURFACE: **EXCELLENT**
SCENERY: **MOUNTAINS, LAKES**

The village of Trawsfynydd achieved notoriety in the 1960s, when it became the location of the first Welsh nuclear power station. It's unique in that its water supplies are provided by a lake rather than by sea water. It first started generating power in 1965, but it closed down in 1993, and is currently in the process of being de-commissioned. However, we're not going into the reactor core itself to start this trip, so there's no danger of your leathers glowing in the dark when you get home. Instead, turn right off the A470 just south of the village itself onto the A4212 and head for Bala. The road has a good surface and heads off down Cwm Prysor through some excellent sweeping bends with mountains on either side.

With the 2,800 ft. peak of Arenig Fawr on the right, the road sweeps left and then runs around Llyn Celyn, following the shore closely so it's a bit narrower on this section. With the lake left behind on the right, there's a straightforward run for the last few miles to the junction with the A494. Turn right here for the last couple of hundred yards into the busy centre of Bala where there's plenty of parking and places to eat and drink. The town is an excellent sailing and fishing centre, based upon the 4½ mile long Llyn Tegid, as well as being the centre for Methodism and the original home of the Welshmen who emigrated to South America in 1865 and founded a colony in Patagonia.

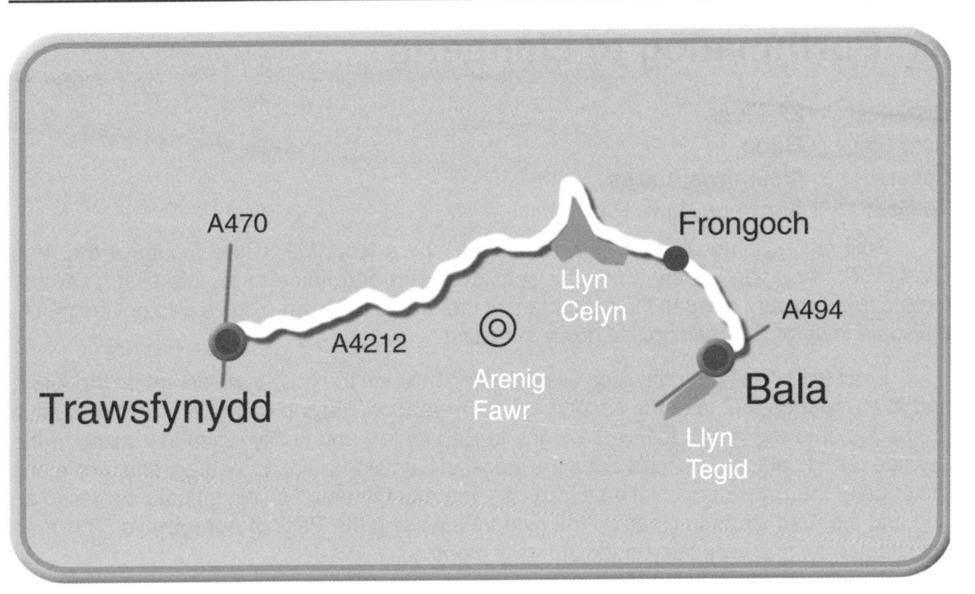

Road	Direction	Comment
A4212	Bala	Turn right off the A470 just south of Trawsfynydd
A494	Bala	Turn right at the junction with the A494 into the town centre

41. Porthmadog to Llanberis

Distance: 22 Miles
Surface: Good
Scenery: Mountains, Lakes
To See: Snowdon, Llyn Padarn

Built on reclaimed land in the 19th century by a local MP at the mouth of the Afon Glaslyn, Porthmadog is now a popular seaside resort and home to an interesting car and motorcycle museum close to the old pottery at the rear of the town. You've also got the mock-Italianate town of Portmeirion just down the coast.

From the bridge over the Afon Glaslyn head through the busy town centre on the A487, and at the roundabout take the second exit to Tremadoc, staying on the A487. Turn right in Tremadoc onto the A498, follow the signs to Beddgelert and finally leave the bustle of the seaside resort behind. The road skirts the massive flats of the Glaslyn estuary and runs along the edge of the Snowdonia National Park. At Nantmor the estuarial plain finally comes to an end and the road starts to climb up the river valley along the Pass of Aberglaslyn. This road is quite narrow and very busy in the summer months.

There's a T-junction in Beddgelert where you should turn right and continue on the A498 - unless you want to stop and look at the priory and the dog's grave that is! Staying with the course of the Afon Glaslyn, the road heads northeast, climbing the flanks of Snowdon which is the big mountain on your left, and running along the northwestern shore of Llyn Dinas. The mountain scenery here is really something else, and the road ain't bad either!

Crossing the valley floor, the road then runs along the opposite shore of Llyn Gwynant before climbing up out of the valley to the junction with the A4086. There's the remains of a Roman camp here and also the Pen-y-Gwrd Inn, which also doubles as a mountain rescue post and was used as a training base for the successful assault on Everest in 1953. Turn left at the junction for the rest of the climb up the Llanberis Pass. The road hugs the flank of the mountain and is very narrow and twisty. It's also very busy in the summer months and some of the traffic doesn't move too quickly either. Keep a special look out for tour coaches on the wrong side of the road as they struggle to get round the tight bends.

After climbing to 1,160 ft., the road heads off down to Llanberis. It's very twisty, there are extremely unforgiving stone walls on each side, the surface is good in places but bumpy in others and it's very busy in the season. The trick is to make the journey at the start or end of the day, and if you want to take the train up to the summit of Snowdon then it's got to be first thing in the morning. Turn up to buy a ticket after 11:00 am and you could be waiting four hours to catch the train!

Llanberis itself doesn't have a lot going for it. It's totally geared for the tourist trade and to extract every penny from them that it can. Double-yellow lines abound, along with traffic wardens to enforce them, and everything's about twice the price that you'd expect to pay elsewhere. If you want to take a break, continue on the A4086 towards Caernarfon and there's a little cafe on the outskirts of the town with plenty of room to park.

This is a cracking road that runs through stupendous scenery. Make the trip early or late in the day to avoid the holiday hordes and the traffic. You have been warned!

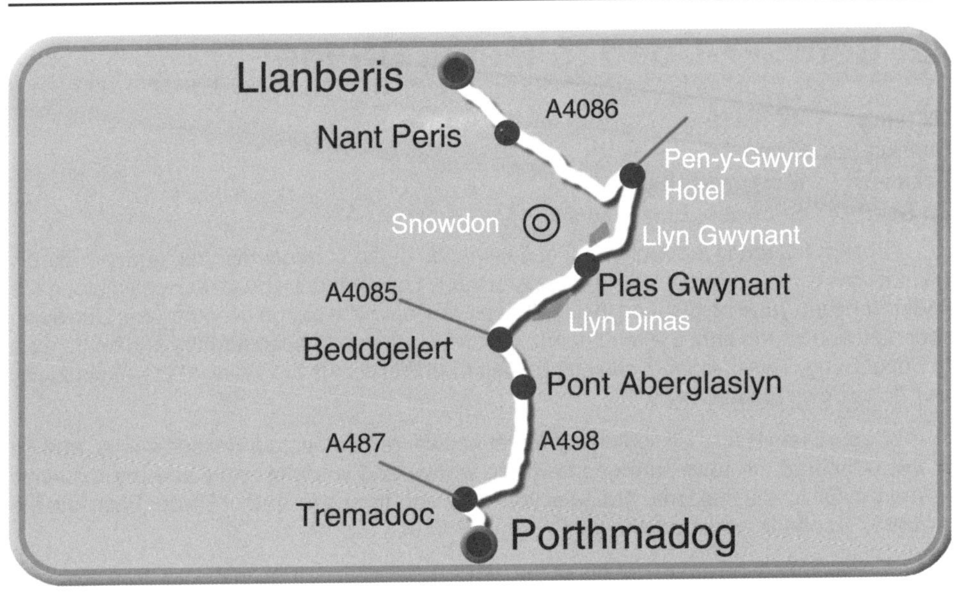

Road	Direction	Comment
A487	Tremadoc	At the roundabout take the second exit to Tremadoc
A498	Beddgelert	Turn right onto the A498 at Tremadoc
A498		At the hotel turn left onto the A4086
A4086	Llanberis	Follow the road to Llanberis. If you want to take a break continue on to the outskirts of Llanberis where there is a cafe with reasonable prices

42. Betws-Y-Coed to Menai Bridge

Distance: 22 Miles
Surface: Good
Scenery: Mountains, Lakes
To See: Snowdon, Llyn Padarn

Betws-Y-Coed is a popular tourist destination in the summer months, and the narrow A5 that runs through the centre can get particularly congested. If you've struggled along the A5 this far, then you'll be pleased to hear that as you leave the bridge over the Afon Llugwy on your right and head north, the road opens out as it climbs up through forestry and bears west to Capel Curig. This is a good, sweeping open road that climbs the valley of the Afon Llugwy as it flows down to the Conwy.

Capel Curig is a small settlement better known for its Mountain Rescue centre, and it's at this point that the road emerges from the woods and you can really see the mountain scenery in full for the first time. Ahead of you is the southwestern spur of Glyder Fach and the A4086 to Llanberis joins from the left.

Carry straight on along the A5 as the road continues its climb up the northeastern side of the Llugwy river valley. The scenery on each side is spectacular and the road surface good, but a bit narrow in places as it struggles round rocky outcrops. And there's some serious drops off to the left!

The Llugwy passes under the road and heads off to up to its source in the mountains on the right, just before the summit of the pass is reached at a little over 1,000 ft., and then the road runs around Llyn Ogwen before descending in a cracking run down the flank of Carnedd Dafydd and into the valley of Nant Ffrancon.

On the other side of the valley are the massive workings of the Penrhyn Slate Quarries, and as the road passes through Bethesda and Tregarth you'll see more evidence of the intensive quarrying and mining activities that have taken place in this area since the 16th century, although it was not until the latter part of the 18th century that the landowners began to develop the quarries and workings. However, slate working has always been carried out on a smaller scale than the mining of coal in the south of Wales.

From here it's a short fast run up to the roundabout at the junction with the A55. Take the first exit to stay on the A5 and follow the dual-carriageway road to the Menai Straits crossing. As soon as you're over the bridge, take the next exit onto the A4080 and then turn right opposite the Carreg Bran Hotel towards Menai Bridge on Ffordd Caergybi. At the next roundabout take the second exit into Cil-Bedlam and follow this road down to the T-junction in the town centre.

The town of Menai Bridge grew out of the communities of Porthaethwy that provided the ferry services between the mainland and the Isle of Anglesey. The opening of Telford's suspension bridge in 1826 saw the end of the ferries, and during the Victorian age the town became a popular resort on the coastal steamer route and a gateway into Anglesey.

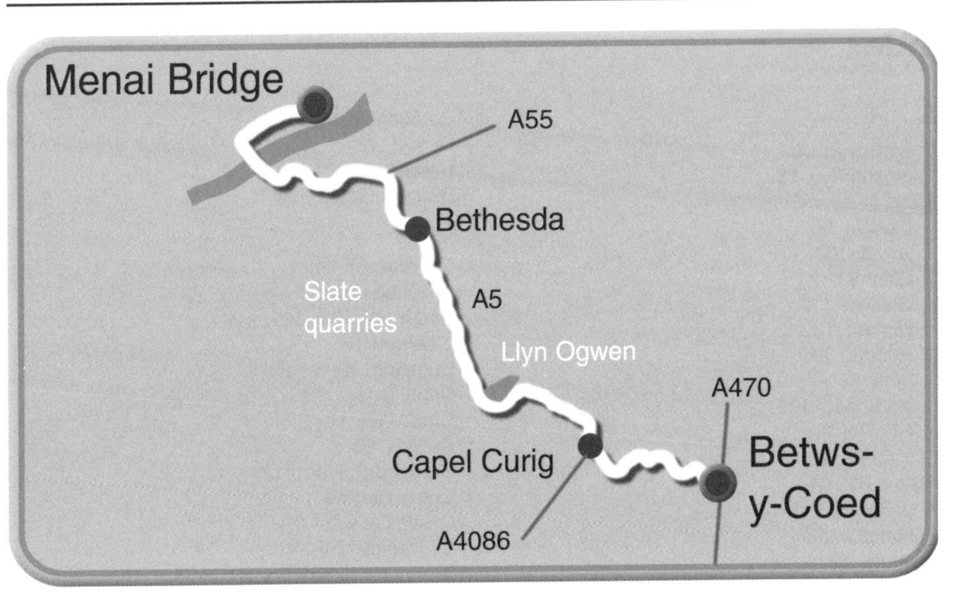

Road	Direction	Comment
A5	Capel Curig	Follow the A5 along the river
A5	Menai Bridge	Follow the A5 all the way to the A55 roundabout
A5	Menai Bridge	First left at the roundabout and follow the dual carriageway to the bridge
A4080	Menai Bridge	Over the bridge take the A4080 and turn right opposite the Carreg Bran Hotel
		At the next roundabout take the second exit to the town centre

Index

A

Abergwesyn 90
Abergynolwyn 98
Afon
- Berwyn 90
- Dinas 102
- Elan 92, 94
- Glaslyn 110
- Hirnant 106
- Honddu 88
- Irfon 90
- Nadroedd 106
- Rheidol 92
- Ystwyth 92

Alston 62, 64
Andover 38
Ashbourne 58
Avebury 40
Aysgarth 68

B

Bala 108
Bampton 28
Banbury 46, 48
Barmouth 104
Barnard Castle 62
Bearings 16
Beaufort 84
Beddgelert 110
Bedford 50
Betws-Y-Coed 112
Bicester 44
Bike Spares 16
Bishops Auckland 74
Bishops Lydeard 30
Black Sheep Brewery 70
Blewbury 42
Blood Alcohol 7
Brakes 16
Brecon 86
Brecon & Abergavenny Canal 84
Brecon Beacons 77, 84, 88
Bridgewater 32
Brigstock 52
Bristol Channel 18, 32
Bruton 34
Bryn-Eglws 98
Bryncrug 98
Builth Wells 88
Bum-Bag 15
Burford 46
Burnhope Seat 62
Buscot 42
Bwlch 84
Bwlch-y-Groes 106

C

Caban-coch 94
Cable ties 12
Cader Idris 98, 102, 104
Caerwen 94
Camping 22
Capel Curig 112
Cargo Net 11
Carlisle 66
Carnedd Dafydd 112
Carter Bar 74
Castle Cary 34
Castleside 74
Centre for Alternative Technology 102
Chain Oiling 12
Chain/sprockets 16
Chepstow 80
Cherhill 40
Cheviot Hills 74
Chipping Norton 46
Control Cables 16
Cooling System 16
Corbridge 74
Corby 52
Corris 102
Countisbury 32
Cwmystwyth 92

D

Deddington 48
Devil's Bridge 92
Dinas Mawddwy 100
Dinas Mill 90
Dolgellau 104
Dovey Forest 100
Drainage Museum 54
Dunster Castle 32

E

Ear plugs 11
Early Invaders 1–2
East Witton 70
Elan Valley 77, 92
Elworthy 30
Erlestoke 36
Esgair Ffrwd 90
Esgair Gelli 90

Esgair Graflwyn 96
Exford 30
Exmoor 30, 32

F

Farringdon 42
Featherbed Top 60
First Aid Kit 11
Froxfield 40

G

Garreg-ddu 94
Garrigill 62
Garsdale 68
Garth 86
Glossop 60
Gloves 11
Glyder Fach 112
Grazeley 38
Great West Road 40

H

Hadrian's Wall 74
Hawes 68
Heads of the Valleys 84
High Force 62
Holwick Scars 62
Hungerford 36, 40
Hurstbourne Priors 38

I

International Calls 5
Islip 52

J

Jedburgh 74
Jervaulx Abbey 70

K

Kendal 66
Kidlington 48
Kimbolton 50
Kingsclere 38

L

Lake District 17
Lake Vyrnwy 106
Lambourn Downs 42
Langport 34
Launceston 26
Lechlade 42
Leyburn 70
Lifton 26
Lights
  alignment 16
  spare bulbs 11
Littleport 54
Llanberis Pass 77, 110
Llangorse 84
Llangynidr 84
Llanidloes 96
Llanwrtyd Wells 90
Llanymaddwy 106
Llyn
  Celyn 108
  Clywedog 96
  Dinas 110
  Gwynant 110
  Lockwood 110
  Tegid 108
Locks 12
Long Crendon 44
Long Itchington 48
Lower Chapel 88
Lowstock 52
Lydford 34
Lynmouth 32

M

Machynlleth 96
Market Lavington 36
Marlborough 40
Marston 48
Melmerby 64
Mickleton 62
Middleham 70
Mildenhall 54
Minehead 32
Minffordd 98, 102
Mortimer 38
Motorcycle Museum 77
Mumford 56
Mynydd Eppynt 86, 88

N

Nant-y-Maen 90
Nationality Sticker 11
Newbury 40
Northumberland National Park 74
Norton Fitzwarren 28

O

Okehampton 26
Oldbury Castle 40
Outwell 54
Owen Glendower 96

P

Panniers 13
Pass of Aberglaslyn 110
Peak District National Park 58

Penant 106
Penegoes 100
Penmaenpool 104
Pennines 19, 62
Penrhyn Slate Quarries 112
Penrith 64, 66
Penygarreg 94
Pewsey 36
Porlock 32
Porthmadog 110
Post Offices 5
Postcombe 44
Princethorpe 48
Punctures 11

R

Raglan 82
Reading 38
Rest Stops
  Countisbury 32
  Cross Foxes Hotel 100
  Devil's Bridge 92
  Froxfield 40
  High Force Hotel 62
  Lake Vyrnwy 106
  Llanberis 110
  Lynmouth 32
  Pen-y-bont Hotel 98
  Red Lion Inn 100
  Snake Pass Inn 60
  Tasty Bite Cafe 60
  Trout Inn 42
Rhayader 92,94
Ripon 70
River Thames 42, 46
River Usk 82
Rockingham Motor Speedway 52
Rucksacks 15
Rushall 36
Ryton-on-Dunsmore 48

S

Safety Helmets 7
Savernake Forest 40
Shap 66
Sheffield 60
Shirenewton 80
Silbury Hill 40
Simonsbath 30
Slate Museum
  Abergynolwyn 98
Snake Pass 60
Snowdon Mountain Railway 110
Somerton 34
Southam 48
Spare Keys
Speed Limits 7
Staylittle 96
Streatley 42
Sudbury 52

T

Tadley 38
Tail Packs 15
Tal-y-llyn Railway 98
Talgarth 84
Tank Bags 14
Tank Tape 12
Taunton 28, 30
Thame 44
Thetford 56
Throwover Panniers 14
Top Box 13
Tow Law 74
Trawsfynydd 108
Tregaron 90
Tremadoc 110
Tyres 16
Tywi Forest 90
Tywyn 98

U

Upper Chapel 88
Upwell 54
Urchfont 36
Usk 80

V

Vale of the White Horse 42
Visors 7

W

Wantage 42
Waterrow 28
Watership Down 38
Watersmeet 30
Wensleydale 68
West Grafton 36
West Kennet Long Barrow 40
Westbury 36
Whitchurch 38